Living *Water*

a creative resource for the Liturgy

Prayer of the Faithful

YEAR B

Susan Sayers

with Father Andrew Moore

This edition published in 1999 by
KEVIN MAYHEW LTD
Buxhall
Stowmarket
Suffolk IP14 3BW

Prayer of the Faithful is extracted from
Living Water – Complete Resource Book

0 1 2 3 4 5 6 7 8 9

ISBN 1 84003 404 1
Catalogue No 1500299

Cover photograph courtesy of
Images Colour Library Limited, London
Cover design by Jaquetta Sergeant
Edited by Katherine Laidler
Typesetting by Louise Selfe
Printed and bound in Great Britain

FOREWORD

A praying church is a living organism, powered by the love of God, and directed by his will. The aim of those leading intercessions in public worship is to provide a suitable climate for prayer, both for the faithful core of praying members, and also for those who drift in as visitors, sometimes willingly and sometimes rather grudgingly.

Since our God is in a far better position to know the needs of each muddle of people who arrive on any particular Sunday, it is obviously sensible to prepare for leading the intercessions by praying for those who will be there, asking our God to lead us with his agenda in mind, rather than taking immediate charge ourselves. Then we have to give him a chance to answer! You may find that a quiet walk enables you to do this, or a time wandering round the empty church, or time spent on some of the mechanical jobs at home while you still your heart and resist the temptation to badger God with good ideas.

The ideas provided reflect the day's readings, and as you read through them you may well find that these ideas will spark off other thoughts of your own. Do use them however you wish – exactly as they stand, adapted to suit specific needs, or simply as a starting point. They are a resource to help you, not a cage to keep your own ideas out.

During the service be alert to what is being said and how God is moving among you, so that you can pick up on these threads, if it seems appropriate, during the intercessions. And if you have young children present, give some thought to how they can also be praying at this time. They might be following a picture prayer trail, singing a quiet worship song, drawing some situation they are praying for, or looking through the intercession pictures provided in children's communion books.

I have heard it said that since God can hear the prayers, it doesn't really matter if the congregation can't. I don't agree. In public worship it can be very distracting to be straining to hear, or isolating if you can hear only a vague mumble. Do take the trouble to practise speaking clearly and fairly slowly in the church, so that everyone can comfortably take in what you are saying. Bear in mind that nerves usually make us speed up somewhat, so speak extra slowly to allow for this.

Finally, don't recite what you have written, but pray it. Pray it both through the intentions and through the silences. Leading the intercessions carries a great responsibility, but it is also a great privilege.

SUSAN SAYERS
with Father Andrew Moore

CONTENTS

FEASTS OF THE LORD

ORDINARY TIME

SPECIAL FEASTS

First Sunday of Advent

Be alert and watchful; keep yourselves ready.

Celebrant
As we begin a new year in the life of the Church,
we pray to the God who made us.

Reader
We come to the Lord just as we are
and ask that his kingdom may come
to be within us and in this place.
We pray for an increase in faith
that we may become the lights in darkness
that we are called to be.

Silence

O God, keep us awake to you:
and alive to your call.

The signs in our world of hate, distrust and greed
are shown to us clearly every day.
May our eyes see the signs of hope and victory;
the opportunities for loving service,
for encouragement, reassurance and thanksgiving.

Silence

O God, keep us awake to you:
and alive to your call.

May the parenting and befriending
in all our relationships be blessed,
and may our love for one another be increased.
We pray for the humility
to accept guidance and warnings, lovingly given,
and the courage to uphold one another in the faith.

Silence

O God, keep us awake to you:
and alive to your call.

In love, we bring to our prayers
those who are weary
with ongoing pain and weakness,
those who are frail with age
and all who are vulnerable;
May the Lord pour his living strength into their lives
and protect them from all that is harmful.

Silence

O God, keep us awake to you:
and alive to your call.

We pray for all who have come
to the end of their earthly life,
and for those whose lives
feel empty without them.
May the Lord give comfort to the bereaved,
and everlasting peace to all who rest in his love.

Silence

O God, keep us awake to you:
and alive to your call.

With Mary, the Mother of Jesus,
let us pray:
Hail, Mary . . .

In silence, now,
we bring to God our Father
any needs and concerns
known to us personally.

Silence

Celebrant
Lord, our Creator,
we thank you for the wonder of our being,
and ask you to hear our prayers,
through Jesus Christ.
Amen.

Second Sunday of Advent

*John the Baptist prepares the way
for the coming of the Messiah
by helping the people to realign their lives.*

Celebrant
As we gather expectantly in God's presence,
let us pray.

Reader
We pray that God's cleansing and liberating power
may give us the courage and perception
to see ourselves as we really are,
and lead us to true repentance.

Silence

Come, O come, Emmanuel:
come and live in us.

We pray for the world's leaders and all in authority,
that they may lead and govern wisely and honestly,
without corruption and for the common good.

Silence

Come, O come, Emmanuel:
come and live in us.

We pray that every family
may be surrounded and upheld
by God's loving presence,
that conflicts may be healed and needs provided for,
and every act of kindness blessed.

Silence

Come, O come, Emmanuel:
come and live in us.

We pray for reassurance and healing,
hope and patience
for all who are suffering in any way;

for freedom to all imprisoned by hate or guilt,
and for a change of heart to all who need to forgive.

Silence

Come, O come, Emmanuel:
come and live in us.

We pray for those
who have completed their time on earth.
May they know the freedom, joy and fullness
of unending life in heaven.

Silence

Come, O come, Emmanuel:
come and live in us.

We make our prayer with Mary,
who prepared a way for the Lord:
Hail, Mary . . .

As God's stillness fills our hearts,
we make our private petitions and thanksgivings.

Silence

Celebrant
In great thankfulness
for your compassionate love,
dear Father,
we ask you to accept our prayers,
through Jesus Christ our Lord.
Amen.

THIRD SUNDAY OF ADVENT

In Jesus, God will be fulfilling
the Messianic prophecies about the promised Saviour.

Celebrant
Let us pray now to the living God,
who always keeps his promises,
and who knows us so well.

Reader
May the Church always be faithful
in telling the good news, comforting the desolate,
actively loving justice
and drawing many to freedom
through the joy of the Father's loving forgiveness.

Silence

Keep us faithful, Lord:
to your calling.

As the Church, we pray for the world,
that there may be integrity in leadership;
mercy and justice for rich and poor,
strong and weak;
that there may be peace among nations
and respect for all.

Silence

Keep us faithful, Lord:
to your calling.

As the family of believers, we pray
for those around us now and their needs;
and for the families we represent, and their needs.
May the love of Christ be shown in what we do
and how we speak and how we spend.

Silence

Keep us faithful, Lord:
to your calling.

In compassion we call to mind
all who are locked in physical or emotional pain,
all who are weighed down with worry,
guilt or despair.
Restore and refresh them, comfort and free them.

Silence

Keep us faithful, Lord:
to your calling.

As resurrection people,
we commend to the Father's love
those who have died to this earthly life.
May they, and we in our turn, experience for ever
the joy of eternal life.

Silence

Keep us faithful, Lord:
to your calling.

With Mary,
who mothered the Son of God,
we make our prayer:
Hail, Mary . . .

In the knowledge
that God wants our spiritual happiness,
let us pray our private petitions.

Silence

Celebrant
As part of your generous creation, Father,
we give you thanks and praise,
and ask you to accept these prayers,
through Christ Jesus.
Amen.

FOURTH SUNDAY OF ADVENT

*God's promised kingdom,
announced both to King David in ancient times
and to Mary by the angel Gabriel, will go on for ever.*

Celebrant
Gathered as the Church of God in this place,
let us pray together for the coming of the kingdom.

Reader
We pray that the Church
may be quiet enough to hear God's voice,
humble enough to move in God's way,
and excited enough to spread the good news.

Silence

Living God:
let your kingdom come.

We pray that all who lead
may do so with integrity and respect for others;
that those in positions of authority
may be blessed with humility and a sense of right;
that unjust practices may be changed for good
and conflicts of great tension be peacefully resolved.

Silence

Living God:
let your kingdom come.

May our homes be places
of loving acceptance and developing faith;
in all our friendships may we learn
to grow in generosity of spirit.

Silence

Living God:
let your kingdom come.

When the waiting is long and painful,
may all who have to wait
be given patience and courage;
may those who are wounded,
whether physically or emotionally,
be granted healing
and the assurance of God's presence.

Silence

Living God:
let your kingdom come.

May those who have died to this life,
and whose hope is in the Lord,
be welcomed into eternity.
May those who mourn them be comforted,
and their pain be touched by the divine love.

Silence

Living God:
let your kingdom come.

Remembering Mary's humble acceptance
of God's will,
we join our prayers with hers:
Hail, Mary . . .

The God of Peace is listening;
in this silence we name those we know
who are in any particular need.

Silence

Celebrant
Heavenly Father, accept our prayers,
and make us channels of your peace,
through the power of Jesus Christ.
Amen.

CHRISTMAS DAY

Jesus Christ, the world's Saviour,
is here with us, born as a human baby.

Celebrant
As we gather to celebrate Christmas,
let us pray to the living God.

Reader
With gratitude for our Church and its people,
for our deacons, priests and bishops,
and all who pray,
may we all be blessed and strengthened
in our service,
so we can touch the world with your love.

Silence

Holy God:
be born in us today.

We are thankful for the blessings of creation,
for our world and all its beauty.
May we learn God's ways of love and truth,
that his kingdom may grow and flourish.

Silence

Holy God:
be born in us today.

We pray for God's blessing on all those we love –
our families, neighbours and friends,
whether present with us today or far away.
May we all grow closer
in the happiness of human loving and sharing.

Silence

Holy God:
be born in us today.

With gratitude for our own health and strength,
we pray now for help and healing
wherever people ache with pain and sorrow,
loneliness or fear.
May they be blessed in their need
and surrounded with love.

Silence

Holy God:
be born in us today.

We pray for those who have died
and all for whom Christmas
sharpens the loss of loved ones.

Silence

Holy God:
be born in us today.

We make our prayer with Mary,
in whom the Word was made flesh:
Hail, Mary . . .

We name in this silence
any known to us
with particular needs or burdens.

Silence

Celebrant
Father, we can never thank you enough
for coming to rescue us;
please hear our prayers which we offer
through Jesus, your Son.
Amen.

FIRST SUNDAY OF CHRISTMAS: THE HOLY FAMILY

*The Saviour of the world is born as a fully human baby
into a real human family.*

Celebrant
We are all members of God's family.
Let us pray to him now.

Reader
We pray that our church communities
may reflect the love and mutual care
shown to us in the example of the Holy Family;
that we may recognise our responsibility
to provide spiritual nurture for our young.

Silence

Come, Lord:
and live among us.

We pray for all parents and children,
that our laws and structures of society
may uphold and support them.
We pray for the very poor
and those who struggle to survive.

Silence

Come, Lord:
and live among us.

We pray for the families we know well,
especially those with conflicts or pressures;
may the Holy Spirit protect them
so that each family member
may know they are loved
and grow in love themselves.

Silence

Come, Lord:
and live among us.

We pray for all refugees and war-torn families;
for all children at risk of abuse,
and all families where there is violence.
We pray that the Spirit may bring hope,
healing and transformation.

Silence

Come, Lord:
and live among us.

We pray for those who have died
and for their families who mourn them.
May they receive a merciful judgement
and experience the unending peace of heaven.

Silence

Come, Lord:
and live among us.

We make our prayer with Mary,
Mother of the Church:
Hail, Mary . . .

As members of Christ's family,
we pray to our loving Lord,
who considers each one of us special.

Silence

Celebrant
Heavenly Father, dwell in our hearts and homes,
and accept these prayers through Jesus Christ,
our brother and Redeemer.
Amen.

SECOND SUNDAY OF CHRISTMAS

The Word made flesh at Christmas was always with God,
always expressing his creative love.

Celebrant
Let us pray to the God
who loves us enough to come and save us.

Reader
We pray for the areas of the Church
which are weak in faith,
despondent or complacent;
that we may be recharged
with the power of God's love,
reawakened to the good news,
and revitalised with the breath of the Spirit.

Silence

Living Word of God:
be spoken in our lives.

We pray for all areas of misunderstanding
between peoples and nations,
between needs and offers of help;
make us more ready to listen than instruct,
more ready to encourage than crush.

Silence

Living Word of God:
be spoken in our lives.

We pray for family feuds and difficulties
to be resolved and learnt from;
for the words we speak
to express love and respect,
with true charity and forgiveness.

Silence

Living Word of God:
be spoken in our lives.

We pray for all who have difficulty
hearing and speaking,
reading and writing;
for the oppressed and persecuted
whose voices are silenced,
and for all who have yet to hear
the good news of God's love.

Silence

Living Word of God:
be spoken in our lives.

We pray for those who have died
and those who are dying now;
may the Word of life
encourage them on their journey
and bring them safely to the eternal kingdom.

Silence

Living Word of God:
be spoken in our lives.

We join our prayers with those of Mary,
whose Son has brought us salvation:
Hail, Mary . . .

In a time of silence
we share with God our Father
any needs and burdens
known to us personally.

Silence

Celebrant
Almighty Father, hear our prayers
and make us alert to your response,
through Christ our Lord.
Amen.

THE EPIPHANY OF THE LORD

Jesus, the promised Messiah,
is shown to the Gentile world.

Celebrant
Let us pray to the God who loves us
and knows the terrain we travel.

Reader
We thank God for all those who brought
the good news of Jesus to us,
and all who nourish our faith today.
We pray that the whole people of God
may work in unity and openness
for the coming of God's kingdom.

Silence

Lord God:
we offer you ourselves.

We thank God that salvation is for all people,
and pray for a just and accepting world
where none is rejected, despised
or treated with contempt.

Silence

Lord God:
we offer you ourselves.

We thank God for the privilege of parenting
and of living in communities;
we pray that our homes and churches
may be welcoming and generous-hearted.

Silence

Lord God:
we offer you ourselves.

We thank God for all who care
with such thoughtfulness and practical loving
for those who are vulnerable,
and especially for the very young.
We pray for healing and wholeness,
peace of mind, protection and hope.

Silence

Lord God:
we offer you ourselves.

We thank God for all who have reached
the end of their earthly journey in faith,
that they may be welcomed into your eternity.
May we use the time left to us here
as good stewards of God's gifts.

Silence

Lord God:
we offer you ourselves.

We make our prayer with Mary,
who showed her Son to the Wise Men:
Hail, Mary . . .

Knowing that our loving Father is listening,
we bring our personal petitions to him now.

Silence

Celebrant
In thankfulness, Father,
we offer you our lives
and our prayers,
through Jesus Christ.
Amen.

THE BAPTISM OF THE LORD

Through the Holy Spirit,
Jesus is affirmed at his Baptism as God's beloved Son,
and we too are given the Spirit of God
which affirms us as God's adopted daughters and sons.

Celebrant
Let the Spirit of God in our hearts plead
for the Church and for the world.

Reader
We pray that the Spirit
may fill the Church with such joy in believing
that all Christians overflow with love,
compassion, generosity and humility.

Silence

May the Spirit of God:
fill us to overflowing.

May God's power and justice
fill the arenas of leadership and conflict
with sharpened consciences and with courage,
so that wise decisions are made,
needs met and wrongs righted.

Silence

May the Spirit of God:
fill us to overflowing.

May God's gentleness and truth
fill every home with new insight
and greater understanding.
Break down the divisive barriers
and build up our capacity to love.

Silence

May the Spirit of God:
fill us to overflowing.

May God's attentive caring
fill us with practical compassion;
may all who suffer be heard,
comforted and cared for.
May there be healing for both their situation
and our hardness of heart.

Silence

May the Spirit of God:
fill us to overflowing.

May God's unending being
fill death with life and the dying with hope.
May we all be prepared
for life which lasts for ever.

Silence

May the Spirit of God:
fill us to overflowing.

Mary opened her life
to the loving power of God;
we now make our prayer with her:
Hail, Mary . . .

Conscious of the Holy Spirit among us,
we share with God our Father
our personal burdens, joys and sorrows.

Silence

Celebrant
Father, we rejoice
in your uncompromising love for us,
and ask you to hear our prayers,
through Jesus Christ.
Amen.

First Sunday of Lent

After his Baptism Jesus is led by the Spirit into the wilderness
before returning to proclaim God's kingdom.

Celebrant
As we begin this season of Lent,
let us move off into the desert
to communicate with our God.

Reader
As we come before God
with all our muddled priorities
and conflicting agendas,
we pray that we may be made whole
as the Body of Christ;
that we may have the strength to renounce evil,
and the courage to announce the kingdom of peace.

Silence

With our God:
all things are possible.

With the world's clamour ringing in our ears,
with comfort zones beckoning us,
but the pain of injustice refusing to be shut out,
we pray for the world's healing,
and for an end to all lying and deceit.

Silence

With our God:
all things are possible.

We come with the demands of home, family, work,
and expectations warring in us
for space and attention.
We pray on behalf of those
too busy or too exhausted to pray;
that our daily lives may be washed in peace,
ordered in holiness and lit up with joy.

Silence

With our God:
all things are possible.

We come with the needs and sorrows,
pain and suffering of our brothers and sisters
all over the world, who are aching –
physically, emotionally or spiritually;
we pray that they may be touched
by God's comforting and healing love.

Silence

With our God:
all things are possible.

In this Lenten season,
we come to realign our lives
in the context of eternity,
and to commend to God's love
our own loved ones
who have passed through earthly death
to the life which has no ending.

Silence

With our God:
all things are possible.

Remembering Mary's dedication and love,
we pray with her:
Hail, Mary . . .

We make our private petitions
and thanksgivings
together now in silence.

Silence

Celebrant
Father, we thank you
for showing us the way to abundant life,
and ask you to hear our prayers
through Jesus Christ.
Amen.

SECOND SUNDAY OF LENT

Christ's willingness to face suffering and death,
in order to save us,
proclaims the total sacrificial love of God.

Celebrant
Let us pray to our God
whose glory fills heaven and earth.

Reader
That in focusing our lives and our worship on God
we may increasingly reflect his love and brightness
so that others are drawn to worship him.

Silence

Lord, open our eyes:
to see your glory.

That the world's leaders may be committed
to alleviating unnecessary suffering
and working co-operatively
for the good of all who inhabit this planet.

Silence

Lord, open our eyes:
to see your glory.

That every word we speak
and every meeting we arrange
may further the building of God's kingdom.

Silence

Lord, open our eyes:
to see your glory.

That all who suffer, whether physically,
spiritually, mentally or emotionally,
may know the comfort, healing
and transforming of God's love.

Silence

Lord, open our eyes:
to see your glory.

That those who have died to this earthly life
may share in the glory of heaven.

Silence

Lord, open our eyes:
to see your glory.

With Mary,
who shared her Son's sorrows,
we make our prayer:
Hail, Mary . . .

We pray in silence, now,
for our individual needs and concerns.

Silence

Celebrant
Father, whose character is always full of mercy,
hear our prayers
through the pleading of your Son, Jesus Christ.
Amen.

THIRD SUNDAY OF LENT

God's wisdom may shock us.
Jesus, obedient to God's Law and fulfilling it,
dies a death which, according to the Law, makes him cursed.

Celebrant
As God has called us,
so we have come to pray.

Reader
We pray for the Church, the Body of Christ,
with all its collected gifts and weaknesses;
may we receive the grace to recognise
that in the Spirit we are one,
and curb in us all tendency to division.

Silence

May we hear you, Lord:
and want to obey.

We pray for the world
in all its beauty and richness;
may we have the desire
and the generosity of spirit
to share our planet's food and resources,
to care for its people's well-being,
and to foster peace and justice for all.

Silence

May we hear you, Lord:
and want to obey.

We pray for those we love –
those we see each day and those we miss;
may we cherish one another
as we live the loving way of your commands.

Silence

May we hear you, Lord:
and want to obey.

We pray for all victims of selfish or violent acts,
and for those whose lives are trapped in sin.
We pray for all whose bodies and minds
have difficulty functioning.
May we be more sensitive to their needs.

Silence

May we hear you, Lord:
and want to obey.

We pray for those who have died
and for those who miss their physical presence.
May the Lord have mercy on them;
may they, and we in our turn,
rest in the peace of God's enfolding love.

Silence

May we hear you, Lord:
and want to obey.

We pray with Mary,
our spiritual Mother:
Hail, Mary . . .

As God's stillness fills our hearts,
we name any we know
who especially need our prayer.

Silence

Celebrant
Father, we thank you
for giving us this opportunity to pray,
and ask you to hear us,
through Jesus Christ.
Amen.

Fourth Sunday of Lent

God loves us so much that he is generous with his mercy.

Celebrant
Trusting not in our own worthiness,
but in God's mercy,
let us pray.

Reader
We pray for all who lead worship
and teach the faith to others;
that hearts may be open to receive
the message of spiritual health and life.

Silence

Day by day, O Lord:
may we remember your love.

We pray for all world leaders,
both in their public office
and in their private lives.
We pray for a collective desire for peace
and the courage to uphold right values.

Silence

Day by day, O Lord:
may we remember your love.

We pray for those we live and work with,
that none may be taken for granted
or live in a climate of condemnation;
but that we may all encourage one another in love.

Silence

Day by day, O Lord:
may we remember your love.

We pray for all condemned to death
or long prison sentences;
for those with long-term and debilitating illness;
for all who have been damaged.

Silence

Day by day, O Lord:
may we remember your love.

We pray for those who have died
and those who miss their physical presence;
May they see the fullness of eternal life.

Silence

Day by day, O Lord:
may we remember your love.

Remembering Mary's hopefulness and love,
we make our prayer with her:
Hail, Mary . . .

We pray in silence, now,
for any who especially need our prayer.

Silence

Celebrant
Merciful Father,
you know our deepest needs;
let your will be done in our lives
and in the lives of those for whom we pray,
through Jesus Christ.
Amen.

FIFTH SUNDAY OF LENT

Through Christ's death, full life would come
to people of all nations and generations.

Celebrant
Let us pray to the God who loves us
and understands our needs.

Reader
We pray for all Church leaders,
teachers and pastors,
and all who are being called
into particular ministries, both lay and ordained.
We pray especially for any who are wrestling
with the demands of such a calling,
that they may be given courage
to offer themselves in the Lord's service.

Silence

Let your name be glorified:
let your will be done.

We pray for the nations of the world,
that, in all their plans and actions,
conflicts and disasters;
the Lord may guard the children,
guide the leaders
and give us all his peace.

Silence

Let your name be glorified:
let your will be done.

We pray for those
who are weighed down with suffering,
or imprisoned by their fears.
May their burdens be eased
and may they be given the strength
to bear what cannot be avoided.

Silence

Let your name be glorified:
let your will be done.

We pray that those whose earthly lives have ended
may have mercy and everlasting peace.

Silence

Let your name be glorified:
let your will be done.

With Mary,
whose heart was pierced with sorrow,
we make our prayer:
Hail, Mary . . .

We pray to our heavenly Father
about our own particular concerns.

Silence

Celebrant
Father, with thankful hearts
we offer these concerns
for the Church and for the world,
through Jesus, our Saviour.
Amen.

PALM (PASSION) SUNDAY

*As the Messiah, Jesus enters Jerusalem, knowing that he rides
towards rejection and death in order to save his people.*

Celebrant
As we face up to the costly loving
shown by our God,
let us approach him in humility
and pray to him now.

Reader
We pray that as a Church
we may love God and one another,
and go on loving,
through insult and praise,
through acceptance and rejection,
in the sure knowledge that the Lord is our God.

Silence

Make us strong:
to do your will in all things.

May the kingdoms of this world
soak up the values of God's kingdom;
may their leaders and their peoples
uphold what is right and just,
and establish a social order
which is rooted in Godly love.

Silence

Make us strong:
to do your will in all things.

In all the heartaches and joys
of human relationships,
may we be governed by selfless love,
faithful and forgiving without limit.

Silence

Make us strong:
to do your will in all things.

May all who suffer come to know
the comforting presence and healing power
of God's forgiving love.

Silence

Make us strong:
to do your will in all things.

We pray for all
who are making that last journey of death,
that they may be surrounded with God's peace
and rest in his love for ever.

Silence

Make us strong:
to do your will in all things.

We join our prayers with those of Mary,
Mother of the King of love:
Hail, Mary . . .

Upheld by God's peace,
we pray now in silence
for any needs known to us personally.

Silence

Celebrant
Father, we rejoice
in your companionship and loyalty,
and ask you to hear our prayers,
for the sake of Jesus, our Saviour.
Amen.

EASTER DAY

Jesus is alive;
God's love has won the victory over sin and death.

Celebrant
As we celebrate the risen Christ,
let us pray to the God of life,
in whom we live.

Reader
That the Church of God
may be bursting with new life,
filled with the love
that takes even death in its stride;
that new and mature Christians together,
all in their various ministries,
may work in God's strength
for the coming kingdom.

Silence

You are our God:
who does all things well.

That the inhabitants of our planet
may recognise God's glory all around,
co-operate in the sharing of his gifts,
and cultivate the habit of caring love.

Silence

You are our God:
who does all things well.

That God will bless our homes and families,
our places of work and leisure,
with new life and the hope of new possibilities
touching the ordinary with beauty and joy.

Silence

You are our God:
who does all things well.

That all who feel trapped or imprisoned –
physically, mentally or spiritually –
may feel the stones rolled away
and new light pouring into their lives.

Silence

You are our God:
who does all things well.

That those who have died to this earthly life
may find the fullness of God's eternity,
flooded with the light of his love.

Silence

You are our God:
who does all things well.

With Mary in her Easter joy
we make our prayer:
Hail, Mary . . .

We pray for our own intentions now,
in silence filled with joy.

Silence

Celebrant
Father, in the name of the risen Jesus,
we ask you to bring the hope,
healing and joy of the Resurrection
to all these people for whom we pray.
Amen.

SECOND SUNDAY OF EASTER

*Our faith in the risen Christ
is bound to affect the way we live.*

Celebrant
Knowing that the risen Christ is here among us,
let us pray in his name
for the Church and for the world.

Reader
We pray for God's blessing
on every group of Christians worshipping today
all over the world;
and we pray for all who doubt the truth.
We pray that our hearts may be set ablaze
with love,
and that we may walk as children of light.

Silence

My Lord and my God!
My Lord and my God!

We pray for all the areas of the world
which are torn apart by hatred and violence,
famine, disease, or religious differences;
we pray for an end to war
and a deeper commitment to peace.

Silence

My Lord and my God!
My Lord and my God!

We pray for those who face family rejection
if they become Christians,
and for all families divided by beliefs
or persecuted for their faith.
We pray for the children of our church
that they may grow up strong in the faith
with good role models to guide them.

Silence

My Lord and my God!
My Lord and my God!

We pray for those who wake up
to the prospect of another day filled with pain;
for those who long for someone
to spend time with them, enjoying their company;
and we pray for sight that notices needs.

Silence

My Lord and my God!
My Lord and my God!

We pray for those who mourn,
and we pray for those they love and miss,
commending all who have died
to the everlasting arms of the God of love,
in whom there is life in all its fullness.

Silence

My Lord and my God!
My Lord and my God!

We make our prayers with those of Mary,
whose trust made our salvation possible:
Hail, Mary . . .

In the silence of God's attentive love,
we name our particular petitions.

Silence

Celebrant
Trusting in your immense compassion, Father,
we offer you our prayers
and ask you to hear us,
through Jesus Christ.
Amen.

THIRD SUNDAY OF EASTER

Having redeemed us by his death,
Jesus can offer us the forgiveness of our sin,
which sets us free to live.

Celebrant
May God be glorified now,
as we commit ourselves to the work of prayer,
interceding for those in all kinds of need.

Reader
In our worship,
and our openness to the Spirit of life,
in the Church's longing and outreach,
in the priests, the people,
in all seekers and honest doubters,
we pray that,

in all this:
God may be glorified.

Silence

In the welfare programmes
and peace-making missions,
in the struggle to uphold justice,
in the aid given to the hungry and homeless,
we pray that,

in all this:
God may be glorified.

Silence

In the loving and costly commitment
of mothers and fathers, brothers and sisters,
daughters and sons,
in the determination to forgive and forgive,
in all the lives shared and cherished,
we pray that,

in all this:
God may be glorified.

Silence

In the work of nursing, comforting and healing,
in the daily patient struggle
with pain and weakness,
and in the practical, good-humoured caring,
we pray that,

in all this:
God may be glorified.

Silence

In the twilight years and the facing of death,
in lives well lived and now breaking into eternity,
we pray that,

in all this:
God may be glorified.

Silence

With Mary, Mother of our Redeemer,
we make our prayer:
Hail, Mary . . .

We name in silence now,
any known to us
with particular needs or burdens.

Silence

Celebrant
Heavenly Father,
slow to anger and quick to forgive,
immerse us in your Spirit
and let your will be done in our lives,
through Jesus Christ.
Amen.

FOURTH SUNDAY OF EASTER

*'I am the Good Shepherd
and I lay down my life for the sheep.'*

Celebrant
The Lord is our Shepherd;
knowing his care for us, let us pray.

Reader
We pray for all who shepherd others
as bishops and pastors,
and for all in their care;
for Christians threatened and under attack;
and all whose ministry feels demanding.
For a greater affection and care, one for another, in the Church.

Silence

The Lord is our Good Shepherd:
there is nothing we shall lack.

We pray for all in positions of leadership
and influence in our world,
that they may use that power for good;
for an increase in our concern
for one another's well-being, across all barriers,
and for all who are working to build community.

Silence

The Lord is our Good Shepherd:
there is nothing we shall lack.

We pray for those who are wandering, lost and aimless,
with no idea that any Good Shepherd exists;
for those who die unaware that they are precious
and valued by the God who loved them into being.

Silence

The Lord is our Good Shepherd:
there is nothing we shall lack.

We pray for those who have died
to this earthly life,
that the Good Shepherd,
who understands what it is to die,
may bring them safely home.

Silence

The Lord is our Good Shepherd:
there is nothing we shall lack.

We pray with Mary,
Mother of the Good Shepherd:
Hail, Mary . . .

In the silence of God's accepting love,
we pray our individual petitions.

Silence

Celebrant
Loving Lord, we thank you
for this opportunity to pray,
and ask you to answer our prayers
in the way that is best for us.
In the name of Jesus we pray.
Amen.

FIFTH SUNDAY OF EASTER

To produce fruit we need to be joined on to the true vine.

Celebrant
Let us pray to the Lord God Almighty,
in whom we live and move and have our being.

Reader
We want to produce good fruit in abundance;
we pray that God may nurture us
as branches of the true vine,
train and prune us where necessary,
and that our spiritual harvest may make rich wine,
wine of the kingdom.

Silence

Your kingdom, let it come!
Your will, let it be done!

We see around our world
the tragic and expensive consequences
of branches cut off from the true vine.
We pray for a seeking after the truth
and a desire to act rightly and justly
in all areas of human society.

Silence

Your kingdom, let it come!
Your will, let it be done!

We pray for those to whom we are linked
by family, friendships or work;
especially we pray for those
separated from their loved ones or their home.

Silence

Your kingdom, let it come!
Your will, let it be done!

We long for healing and wholeness
in all who suffer
and in all dysfunctional communities;
may we be guided to understand
how we might be part of the healing.

Silence

Your kingdom, let it come!
Your will, let it be done!

We know that death cannot separate us
from God's love;
in that knowledge
we commend to God's loving keeping
those who have died and all who miss them.

Silence

Your kingdom, let it come!
Your will, let it be done!

With Mary, Mother of the true vine,
we make our prayer:
Hail, Mary . . .

Confident in God's welcoming love,
we pray in silence now
for our individual needs.

Silence

Celebrant
Merciful Father, fulfil our needs
according to your loving wisdom,
through Jesus Christ.
Amen.

Sixth Sunday of Easter

We are to love one another as Jesus loves us.

Celebrant
Knowing God's love and affection for us,
let us pray to him now.

Reader
Wherever there is friction and conflict
in the Church,
and communities are divided and weakened;
may we have a greater longing for God's healing
and a deeper commitment to his forgiving love.

Silence

Help us, Lord:
to love one another.

Wherever tangled political situations
seem impossible to solve,
wherever conflicting interests threaten peace;
wherever the ears of the powerful
remain insulated against the cries of the oppressed;
may we have ears to hear the Spirit's guidance.

Silence

Help us, Lord:
to love one another.

Wherever families are dysfunctional
or children are in danger;
wherever the daily living conditions
are damaging to health and self-respect;
may God's kingdom come.

Silence

Help us, Lord:
to love one another.

Wherever the ill and injured
need comfort and assistance;
wherever the elderly and housebound
sit each day for hours alone;
may we bring love and help.

Silence

Help us, Lord:
to love one another.

Wherever people are travelling
that last journey of death,
may they be surrounded by God's love
and welcomed into heaven,
and may those who mourn be comforted.

Silence

Help us, Lord:
to love one another.

Mary's example teaches us
the power of loving response;
with her we make our prayer:
Hail, Mary . . .

Surrounded by God's love,
we pray in silence for our own needs.

Silence

Celebrant
Heavenly Father,
so unrestrictive in your mercy,
accept our prayers and fulfil our needs,
through Jesus Christ.
Amen.

The Ascension of the Lord

Having bought back our freedom
with the giving of his life,
Jesus enters into the full glory to which he is entitled.

Celebrant
Rejoicing that Jesus has ascended into the heavens,
let us pray in confidence to God our Father.

Reader
We pray in thankfulness
for those who introduced us to Jesus
and who help us along our spiritual journey.
We pray for one another in this church
and for all Christians, young and old,
throughout the world.

Silence

Let the kingdom come:
let your kingdom come.

We pray with longing
for the world to be governed
in accordance with the law of love;
that all creation may be reverenced
and treated with respect.

Silence

Let the kingdom come:
let your kingdom come.

We pray with concern
for all the homes, schools and places of work
in this community;
rejoicing in all that is of God,
and asking for healing forgiveness
wherever there is discord or bitterness.

Silence

Let the kingdom come:
let your kingdom come.

We pray with hope
for the healing and restoration to wholeness
of all who are ill or troubled,
damaged or depressed.

Silence

Let the kingdom come:
let your kingdom come.

We pray with confidence
for those who have come to the end
of their earthly lives,
that they may be given merciful judgement
and welcomed into the glory of heaven.

Silence

Let the kingdom come:
let your kingdom come.

We pray with Mary,
sharing her joy at her Son's Ascension:
Hail, Mary . . .

In silence now,
we bring to our heavenly Father
our own particular concerns.

Silence

Celebrant
God of all mercy,
our hope and our joy,
we ask you to hear our prayers,
through Christ Jesus.
Amen.

SEVENTH SUNDAY OF EASTER

Although now hidden from our sight,
Jesus lives for ever, and in him we can live
the Resurrection life even while we are on earth.

Celebrant
Let us pray together to our heavenly Father,
knowing his love for us.

Reader
As the Church,
we are called to do God's will,
to live his way
and to serve one another in love.
We pray that we may be empowered
to do this.

Silence

Lord, we wait on you:
fill us, Holy Spirit of God.

We pray that our states and kingdoms
may display love, truth, justice and mercy,
that the walls of prejudice may be broken
and bridges of reconciliation and trust be built.

Silence

Lord, we wait on you:
fill us, Holy Spirit of God.

May our children be safely and lovingly nurtured,
our elderly valued,
our homes be places of welcome and warmth.

Silence

Lord, we wait on you:
fill us, Holy Spirit of God.

We pray for healing
for those whose lives are aching and weary;

for comfort and reassurance
for all who are imprisoned by fears and hate.

Silence

Lord, we wait on you:
fill us, Holy Spirit of God.

We commit our loved ones who have died
into God's safe keeping for ever.
May we all be worthy to enter eternal life.

Silence

Lord, we wait on you:
fill us, Holy Spirit of God.

We pray with Mary,
Mother of the Church:
Hail, Mary . . .

In the knowledge that God is listening,
we make our private petitions
and thanksgivings.

Silence

Celebrant
Trusting in your love for us, Father,
and full of hope in your promise to hear us,
we offer you these prayers,
in the name of Jesus Christ, your Son.
Amen.

PENTECOST

*The Holy Spirit of God is poured out in power
on the expectant disciples, just as Jesus promised.*

Celebrant
In the power of the Holy Spirit,
let us pray.

Reader
For a fresh in-breathing of life and power
in each church community,
which breaks down our barriers
and sets us on fire with God's love.

Silence

Come, Holy Spirit:
Holy Spirit, come!

For the grace to see this world
and its needs and problems
through the eyes of love, hope,
justice and mercy;
for the grace to abandon prejudice
and build bridges of reconciliation.

Silence

Come, Holy Spirit:
Holy Spirit, come!

For the Spirit of loving kindness
to fill our homes, schools and places of work;
for family rifts to be healed
and long-standing conflicts resolved.

Silence

Come, Holy Spirit:
Holy Spirit, come!

For the restoration of those who are sick
to wholeness and well-being;

for courage and patience in all suffering,
and for good to be distilled
from every painful, destructive experience.

Silence

Come, Holy Spirit:
Holy Spirit, come!

For God's merciful judgement
on those who have died,
and the opportunity for us all
to prepare carefully for meeting God
face to face.

Silence

Come, Holy Spirit:
Holy Spirit, come!

We join our prayers with those of Mary,
who joyfully received the Holy Spirit:
Hail, Mary . . .

Refreshed in the Holy Spirit,
we approach our loving Father
with our private petitions.

Silence

Celebrant
Loving Father,
rejoicing in your strength and fellowship,
we lay these prayers before you,
through Jesus Christ.
Amen.

TRINITY SUNDAY

*The mysterious and holy nature of the one true God
is beyond our understanding, but it is both communal harmony
and individual personality, Father, Son and Holy Spirit.*

Celebrant
Let us pray to the Father
through the Son
and in the power of the Holy Spirit.

Reader
May the Church reflect the community and unity
within the Trinity;
may there be Godly harmony, shared ministry,
mutual support and encouragement in the faith.

Silence

May your will be done:
on earth as it is in heaven.

May the world's leaders
seek not personal power but the public good;
may conflicts be faced honestly
and needs recognised and met;
may all our communities be built up
on what is good, true, just and right.

Silence

May your will be done:
on earth as it is in heaven.

May there be love and respect
for one another in every household;
may there be mutual support
and thoughtfulness, consideration and trust.

Silence

May your will be done:
on earth as it is in heaven.

May the hearts' cries for help be heard;
the tears collected and the fears quieted;
may suffering be eased and guilt erased
through your healing love.

Silence

May your will be done:
on earth as it is in heaven.

May the dead rise to new and eternal life,
freed from their aching and restored for ever.

Silence

May your will be done:
on earth as it is in heaven.

Remembering Mary's special vocation,
we make our prayer with her:
Hail, Mary . . .

In silence filled with love,
we pray our individual petitions.

Silence

Celebrant
Heavenly Father,
eternal and always present,
we offer you these prayers
in the name of Jesus.
Amen.

CORPUS CHRISTI

In bread and wine at the Last Supper,
Jesus offers himself, the Lamb of God
who takes away the sins of the world.

Celebrant
Gathered as the Body of Christ,
let us pray together to our heavenly Father.

Reader
We pray for all who celebrate
the Eucharistic mysteries,
all who administer the sacrament
of the body and blood of Christ,
and all who receive it, day by day,
week by week and year by year.
Through the loving nature of this feeding
may we all grow in holiness
and bring God's life to all we meet.

Silence

In our need, Lord:
we come to you.

We pray that all who know
their hunger and thirst for real feeding
may find the spiritual nourishment they crave,
and receive new and satisfying life
through Christ our Lord.
We pray that the world may know God's love for it.

Silence

In our need, Lord:
we come to you.

We pray for the spiritual feeding of our families,
and our parish family, through word and sacrament;
may we daily draw closer to the God who loves us,

and our lives become increasingly filled with his
life as we feed on him.

Silence

In our need, Lord:
we come to you.

We pray for those who, through frailty or illness,
receive the sacrament in their homes or in hospital;
for all who are malnourished or starving,
whether physically, emotionally or spiritually.

Silence

In our need, Lord:
we come to you.

We pray for those who have died,
that in mercy they may be brought
into the eternal joy of heaven.

Silence

In our need, Lord:
we come to you.

We make our prayers with Mary,
who brought the living bread into the world:
Hail, Mary . . .

Let us be still in the presence of God
and bring to him the needs and concerns
that weigh on our hearts.

Silence

Celebrant
Heavenly Father,
you nourish us by the body and blood of Jesus,
so that we can share in the life of heaven,
both now and at the end of time.
Hear our prayers and provide for us all.
Amen.

SECOND SUNDAY OF THE YEAR

Christ calls us to follow him and walk his way through our lifetime.

Celebrant
Let us pray to the God who has called us to be here,
bringing to him the cares of our Church and our world.

Reader
We pray for deeper faith among Christians,
and a readiness to respond to God's calling.
For those being called to particular ministries
and those called to change their way of living,
we pray for courage, and the grace to obey.

Silence

Unfailing love is yours, Lord:
you are our rock of refuge.

We pray for all who feel pressurised
to conform to wrong values
in order to be accepted;
for a commitment to fight evil
and cultivate good in our world.

Silence

Unfailing love is yours, Lord:
you are our rock of refuge.

We pray for the households of this parish
and God's indwelling there;
for guidance in the everyday decisions
and the times of crisis.

Silence

Unfailing love is yours, Lord:
you are our rock of refuge.

We pray for the weak, the vulnerable,
the weary and the desolated;

for those entrenched in sin
and endangering others.

Silence

Unfailing love is yours, Lord:
you are our rock of refuge.

We pray for those who have died
in God's friendship,
and give thanks for their lives.
May they be called into the light of heaven.

Silence

Unfailing love is yours, Lord:
you are our rock of refuge.

We make our prayer with Mary,
who lovingly made herself available
to God's will:
Hail, Mary . . .

In silence filled with love,
we name our particular prayer burdens.

Silence

Celebrant
Loving Father,
we thank you for calling us,
and ask you to hear these prayers we offer,
through Christ, our Saviour.
Amen.

THIRD SUNDAY OF THE YEAR

When we are called we need to respond with obedience
so that many may be brought to repentance.

Celebrant
Through the faithfulness of others
we have heard the good news.
In thankfulness, let us pray.

Reader
We thank God for all who have worked
to spread the good news in every generation,
so that we have been able to hear it.
May we, too, be faithful in passing on
the Gospel of God's love and forgiveness.

Silence

Make us lights:
to shine in the world.

We thank God for all
who have answered the call to repentance.
We pray for all peacemakers
and those striving to establish justice,
breaking the cycle of revenge with forgiveness.

Silence

Make us lights:
to shine in the world.

We thank God for every resolved conflict,
every heartfelt apology
and all open-hearted forgiveness.
We pray for all whom we have wronged
and those who have wronged us.

Silence

Make us lights:
to shine in the world.

We thank God
for the strength and wholeness he brings us,
and pray for all who are suffering.
May they be healed and comforted,
and may our hands be ready
to carry out God's loving care.

Silence

Make us lights:
to shine in the world.

We thank God for lives well lived;
for the example of those who have died
in his friendship.
May they come to know the joy of heaven.

Silence

Make us lights:
to shine in the world.

As we open our hearts to receive Jesus,
we remember Mary's receptive love,
and make our prayer with her:
Hail, Mary . . .

In silence we pray to God our Father
for our own intentions.

Silence

Celebrant
Rejoicing that we have been called
to serve you, Father,
we offer you these prayers,
along with our lives for you to use;
through Christ our Lord.
Amen.

Fourth Sunday of the Year

Jesus displays all the signs
that mark him out to be God's chosen One.

Celebrant
As we gather in the presence
of the almighty, all-knowing God,
let us pray.

Reader
May the whole Church honour
and glorify God's holy name
in daily lives, private prayer and public worship.

Silence

Holy God:
may your will be done.

May the whole world resound with God's truth,
activate his compassion,
and be soaked in his peace.

Silence

Holy God:
may your will be done.

May all homes and households
make plenty of room for kindness and forgiveness;
clear the clutter of discontent,
and make us more thankful.

Silence

Holy God:
may your will be done.

May all who ache with sadness or physical pain
be comforted and cherished
by God's love for them.

Silence

Holy God:
may your will be done.

May the dying be surrounded with our prayers,
and those who have passed beyond death
remain safe for ever in God's keeping.

Silence

Holy God:
may your will be done.

With Mary, Mother of the Christian family,
we make our prayer:
Hail, Mary . . .

Now, in the space of silence,
we bring to God our Father
our private petitions.

Silence

Celebrant
Most merciful Father,
we ask you to accept these prayers,
through Jesus Christ.
Amen.

FIFTH SUNDAY OF THE YEAR

The good news about God is far too good to keep to ourselves.

Celebrant
We have gathered in the presence
of the one, holy God,
from whom all things take their being.
Let us pray to him now.

Reader
Wherever the sparkle of our vision has dulled,
may the Lord set us glowing once again
at the very thought of him;
may he restore our longing to draw closer to him
until our lives reflect his shining.

Silence

Who is the King of glory?
It is the Lord our God.

Wherever important and far-reaching decisions
need to be made,
wherever wrongs need righting
and justice needs to be restored,
we pray for the holy breath
of wisdom and integrity.

Silence

Who is the King of glory?
It is the Lord our God.

Wherever ongoing family conflicts need resolving,
wherever communication has broken down,
we pray for the capacity for unconditional loving,
and appreciation of every 'other'
as another child of the Father's creating.

Silence

Who is the King of glory?
It is the Lord our God.

Wherever there is pain and suffering,
whether physical, emotional, mental or spiritual,
we pray for a fulsome and holy healing,
and ask for the courage and strength
to make ourselves available
and ready to help.

Silence

Who is the King of glory?
It is the Lord our God.

As we call to mind those who have recently died
and those who will die today,
we pray for each of them,
that in their dying
they may find the greatest healing of all,
as they come into the Father's holy presence for ever.

Silence

Who is the King of glory?
It is the Lord our God.

We join our prayers with those of Mary,
the Mother of our Saviour:
Hail, Mary . . .

Now, in silence,
we pray our individual petitions
to our heavenly Father,
who has promised to hear us.

Silence

Celebrant
Almighty Father, hear the prayers we offer,
and use our bodies, minds and spirits
in establishing your kingdom.
In the name of Jesus we pray.
Amen.

SIXTH SUNDAY OF THE YEAR

Jesus wants to heal us to wholeness,
and to him no one is untouchable.

Celebrant
Let us come to ask for the healing touch of our God
in the Church and in the world.

Reader
The God of humility, in his desire to save us,
was willing to share our human brokenness;
as the Body of Christ, may the Church share
that willingness to be vulnerable
in order to serve in love.

Silence

Good physician:
heal us.

God's power and authority is gracious and merciful;
may all those with authority in our world
be inspired to act with mercy and compassion,
so that the way may be opened
for the kingdom to be established.

Silence

Good physician:
heal us.

May we all have the strength
to drive far from our homes and communities
all rejection and devaluing;
all justification for barriers;
and the courage to reach out in love.

Silence

Good physician:
heal us.

May God's compassion shock us
into seeing more clearly the ache of those
whom society rejects and overlooks;
the wounds of the discarded
and socially embarrassing.
May we reach out where others turn away.

Silence

Good physician:
heal us.

We remember those who, healed for ever,
live with God in the fullness of life.
We pray that we too may come
to share the life which has no ending.

Silence

Good physician:
heal us.

We pray with Mary,
solace and comforter:
Hail, Mary . . .

In silence filled with love,
we pray for those known to us
who need healing.

Silence

Celebrant
Father, your amazing compassion
fills us with wonder;
in joy and thankfulness we offer you
our praise and intercession
through the person of Jesus.
Amen.

SEVENTH SUNDAY OF THE YEAR

The Son of Man has authority on earth to forgive sins.

Celebrant
In the sure knowledge that God cherishes us,
let us pray to him now.

Reader
Our heavenly Father is so full of forgiveness and mercy;
may the Church be filled to the brim with such holiness
that our understanding deepens daily,
and all our work and worship glorifies his name.

Silence

Holy God:
release in us your praise.

Our heavenly Father is so wise and perceptive;
may he give us the grace to share in the healing
between factions and nations,
guided by the Spirit.

Silence

Holy God:
release in us your praise.

Our heavenly Father is so comforting and kind;
may we notice the needs around us,
in our families, friends and colleagues,
and respond to them in love.

Silence

Holy God:
release in us your praise.

We bring to our heavenly Father
our sisters and brothers whose joints are stiff
and whose bodies cannot move freely;
we give thanks for their courage and example;

and pray that God will help their spirits to dance
and fill their hearts with joy.

Silence

Holy God:
release in us your praise.

We commend those who have recently died
to the everlasting care of the Father,
and may those who mourn their going
be comforted.

Silence

Holy God:
release in us your praise.

We make our prayer with Mary,
merciful Mother of Jesus:
Hail, Mary . . .

Confident in God's restoring love,
we pray silently now
for our personal concerns.

Silence

Celebrant
Heavenly Father, so full of power
and yet so personally involved with us,
accept these prayers
and let your will be done in our lives;
through Jesus Christ we pray.
Amen.

EIGHTH SUNDAY OF THE YEAR

*The long-expected bridegroom is Christ,
and the Church is his bride. We cannot half-attend the wedding feast,
but must wholeheartedly join in the celebrations.*

Celebrant
Let us pray to the God of glory,
revealed to us in his Son, Jesus.

Reader
As we listen to the Father's beloved Son,
we pray that we do not fail to hear his will for us
or share his longing for the world to be saved.

Silence

Let us worship the Lord:
in the beauty of holiness.

We pray for an increase in our desire
to enter into one another's suffering and hardship,
to share the world's resources fairly
with one another,
and recognise all humanity as brothers and sisters.

Silence

Let us worship the Lord:
in the beauty of holiness.

We pray for the grace
to not take one another for granted,
but wake each morning ready to notice the Christ
in each person we see and speak to;
and reverence the Father's hidden presence
in all creation.

Silence

Let us worship the Lord:
in the beauty of holiness.

In our prayer we stand alongside
all who are too weak to pray, or too confused;
may all who are suffering
sense the Father's love and comfort,
and be given strength to persevere,
and peace of mind and spirit.

Silence

Let us worship the Lord:
in the beauty of holiness.

We commend to God's eternal presence
those who have recently died,
that they may rest in peace and rise in glory.

Silence

Let us worship the Lord:
in the beauty of holiness.

We make our prayer with Mary,
the chosen one of God:
Hail, Mary . . .

Together in silence,
we name those known to us
who need our prayers.

Silence

Celebrant
Father, we have so often experienced
your loving kindness in our lives;
accept now these prayers and answer them
in the way that is best for your creation,
through Christ our Lord.
Amen.

Ninth Sunday of the Year

Jesus has the words of eternal life –
he sheds light on a right attitude to the Law.

Celebrant
Through Jesus
we are shown God's compassion and mercy;
let us pray to the Father for that love in our lives,
in the Church and in the world.

Reader
Let compassion and mercy
be the hallmarks of our church life
and all its activities;
may they shine in all our behaviour,
our conversations and activities.

Silence

Lord of love:
let only your will be done.

Let compassion and mercy
take root in every institution, policy and structure;
let them challenge accepted wrongs
and disturb complacency.

Silence

Lord of love:
let only your will be done.

Let compassion and mercy
guard every doorway and fill every room;
let them colour each encounter
and drive every decision.

Silence

Lord of love:
let only your will be done.

Let compassion and mercy
transform our attitudes
to all whose illness or frailty
makes them marginalised, ignored or despised.
Let there be healing of all damaged self-perception,
and restoration of jarred human dignity.

Silence

Lord of love:
let only your will be done.

Let compassion and mercy
accompany the dying
and welcome them into eternity.

Silence

Lord of love:
let only your will be done.

We join our prayers with those of Mary,
Mother of the Lord of the Sabbath:
Hail, Mary . . .

To the Lord who brings us life,
we pour out our private petitions
and thanksgivings.

Silence

Celebrant
In praise and gratitude
we offer you these prayers, Father,
through Jesus Christ.
Amen.

Tenth Sunday of the Year

*Anyone who does God's will
is considered a close family member of Jesus.*

Celebrant
As members of God's family,
let us pray together to our heavenly Father.

Reader
That as family members of the Church of God
we may show his likeness by doing his will;
that those visiting our churches
may find there God's beauty and truth,
open-hearted loving and a unity of purpose.

Silence

Father:
let your will be done.

That as members of the human race
we may work together, share resources,
respect and learn from one another.
That leaders may inspire collective good,
and those with vision be valued and heard.

Silence

Father:
let your will be done.

That we may give both support and space
to those we love and nurture;
that those of our own families
who do not yet know God
may come to understand the depth
of his love for them.

Silence

Father:
let your will be done.

That all who come to Jesus in need
may find in him forgiveness, healing
and wholeness of body, mind and spirit,
strength to cope with their difficulties
and a constant inner renewing.

Silence

Father:
let your will be done.

That as those coming to death
roll up the tents of their earthly existence,
they may be welcomed into the eternal home
prepared for them by their loving God.

Silence

Father:
let your will be done.

We pray now with Mary,
whose willing obedience
made our salvation possible:
Hail, Mary . . .

In silence, now,
we approach our loving Father
with our private petitions.

Silence

Celebrant
Most merciful Father,
who knows us so well,
accept our prayers
through Christ Jesus.
Amen.

ELEVENTH SUNDAY OF THE YEAR

From small beginnings, and by God's power,
the kingdom of heaven grows.

Celebrant
Let us pray to the God of heaven and earth
for the growth of the kingdom.

Reader
May the kingdom grow
in clusters of Christians all over the world;
may it grow as hearts are warmed
by encounter with the living God;
nourished by word and sacrament,
private prayer and public worship.

Silence

Lord of heaven:
let the kingdom grow!

May the kingdom grow
in states, empires and monarchies,
in the crowded streets of cities
and in the scattered rural communities;
in all decision-making and all spending.

Silence

Lord of heaven:
let the kingdom grow!

May the kingdom grow
in every human shelter and home,
every place of work and education,
in each conversation and
in our mutual care of one another.

Silence

Lord of heaven:
let the kingdom grow!

May the kingdom grow
to bring peace and healing
wherever there is pain or sadness;
to bring reassurance, comfort, courage and hope.

Silence

Lord of heaven:
let the kingdom grow!

In the knowledge that we must all face judgement,
we pray for those who have died,
thanking God for his loving mercy,
and entrusting our loved ones
to God's safe keeping.

Silence

Lord of heaven:
let the kingdom grow!

We pray with Mary,
who nurtured our Lord in his earthly life:
Hail, Mary . . .

Knowing that God our Father is listening,
we pray in silence
for our own needs and cares.

Silence

Celebrant
Father, we lay our needs and cares before you,
and ask you to hear us,
through Christ.
Amen.

TWELFTH SUNDAY OF THE YEAR

What kind of person is this?
Even the wind and waves obey him.

Celebrant
As residents of God's universe,
let us pray now to our loving Creator.

Reader
We pray for those in positions of authority
in the Church all over the world
and in each gathered community;
that in all the storms
we may be enabled to hear God's calming voice
and deepen our trust in him.

Silence

Lord of all truth and goodness,
calm our fears:
and teach us your peace.

We pray for those with political and military power,
and all whose decisions affect many lives.
May they speak the Spirit's truth into motives,
the Son's honour into actions,
and the Father's vision of peace into every conflict.

Silence

Lord of great power and majesty,
calm our fears:
and teach us your peace.

We pray for all single people,
couples, communal groups and families,
as they weather their storms
and learn from them;
may all who have the care of others
be given the capacity to bring peace and calm fears.

Silence

Lord of all compassion and mercy,
calm our fears:
and teach us your peace.

We pray for those
whose minds and hearts are in turmoil,
whose lives lurch from crisis to crisis;
for those who find their lives shattered
by illness or injury;
for peace in those threatening storms
and a settling of all anxiety.

Silence

Lord of all healing,
calm our fears:
and teach us your peace.

We pray for those who are dying alone,
unnoticed or unprepared;
we commend those who have died
to God's merciful forgiveness
and eternal tranquillity.

Silence

Lord of eternity,
calm our fears:
and teach us your peace.

We pray with Mary,
who served God fearlessly:
Hail, Mary . . .

Trusting in God our Father,
we name our particular prayer burdens.

Silence

Celebrant
Father, rejoicing that you are in overall charge
of all creation,
we offer these prayers,
through Christ Jesus.
Amen.

Thirteenth Sunday of the Year

God's power can reach even into death and draw out life.

Celebrant
As God has called us by name
out into full, abundant life,
let us lay before him now our concerns
for the Church and for the world.

Reader
May all the built-up layers
of complacency or despondency,
of over-comfortable familiarity
or under-active expectation
be removed from the Church
and from our lives,
until we see again
with the freshness and wonder of deepened faith.

Silence

Lord, we believe:
help our unbelief.

We call to mind societies and systems of our world.
May our assumptions be questioned
and our destructive choices challenged;
may the unnoticed scales of prejudice which blind us
be broken away,
so that our world may increasingly come
under the reign of justice, righteousness and love.

Silence

Lord, we believe:
help our unbelief.

May our pride be replaced with humility
until we learn from young children
the lessons of wonder and trust.
May the childlike be kept as a living flame
in all of us, whatever our age,

and enable us to rediscover God's glory
all around us.

Silence

Lord, we believe:
help our unbelief.

As the sick were brought to Jesus
by their loved ones,
so now in prayer we bring all those
whom we long to be healed.
May they hear the Lord's voice
and sense his touch.

Silence

Lord, we believe:
help our unbelief.

Earth-bound, we grieve
at the loss of loved ones through death;
yet we also rejoice
that they have been called by the Lord
into the fullness of everlasting life.

Silence

Lord, we believe:
help our unbelief.

With Mary who gave us her Son,
we make our prayer:
Hail, Mary . . .

In the silence of God's generous love,
we name those known to us
who need our prayers.

Silence

Celebrant
Father, we thank you
for drawing us here to pray,
and ask you to hear us,
through Jesus Christ.
Amen.

Fourteenth Sunday of the Year

If we are not ready to listen to the truth, we will not hear it.

Celebrant
God has drawn us down many different routes
to this shared worship today.
Let us still our bodies
and alert our minds and hearts in his presence.

Reader
We are the Body of Christ
because the Spirit binds us together.
We pray for a real concern and love for one another,
supportive and encouraging,
without malice or bickering,
so that we can be sent out
strong in our weakness and littleness.

Silence

Heavenly Father, give us your grace:
to hear your word with joy.

All the kingdoms and states
are answerable to divine authority,
and much evil is allowed to flourish
through the silence of good people;
we pray for the courage to speak out the truth,
whether it is popular or not.

Silence

Heavenly Father, give us your grace:
to hear your word with joy.

May all our listening
at home, on the phone, at school and at work
be done with our full attention to God's voice
and to one another,
happy to grow wiser through each conversation.

Silence

Heavenly Father, give us your grace:
to hear your word with joy.

We pray for those
whose pain screams silently and incessantly;
for those who have no one to confide in,
no one to listen.
May the love of the Lord enfold them,
his peace calm them
and his healing transform them.

Silence

Heavenly Father, give us your grace:
to hear your word with joy.

In all our life and in all our living
may we be prepared for the life to come;
we commend to the Lord's keeping all those
who have recently made their journey through death.

Silence

Heavenly Father, give us your grace:
to hear your word with joy.

Mary showed us how to listen;
we join our prayers with hers:
Hail, Mary . . .

We bring our personal petitions now
to God our Father, who hears us.

Silence

Celebrant
Father, we ask you to fulfil our prayers
to your glory;
in Jesus' name we pray.
Amen.

FIFTEENTH SUNDAY OF THE YEAR

*Those who speak out God's will
are bound to be vulnerable to rejection and abuse.*

Celebrant
In humility and love
let us draw near to our God
and pray to him now.

Reader
We pray that our lives
may be upright and holy;
that our church communities may shine
with goodness and love, humility and truth;
we pray for all leaning lives to be straightened up
through your merciful forgiveness.

Silence

Holy God, scatter all darkness:
and bathe our world in your light.

We pray that many may be empowered
to recognise evil and fight against it;
to discern warning signs and speak them out;
to notice the sparks of love and goodness
and celebrate them.

Silence

Holy God, scatter all darkness:
and bathe our world in your light.

We pray that our households
and neighbourhoods,
our places of work and leisure,
may be arenas of praise and thankfulness,
not only in the comfort zones
but particularly through the disturbed
and difficult times.

Silence

Holy God, scatter all darkness:
and bathe our world in your light.

We pray for those in prison;
for those leading cruel and violent lives;
for all victims of oppression or abuse;
for all who suffer mental anguish or physical pain.

Silence

Holy God, scatter all darkness:
and bathe our world in your light.

We pray for those who have died,
that they, and we in our turn, may be given
merciful judgement through Jesus our Saviour,
and brought into the unquenchable light of heaven.

Silence

Holy God, scatter all darkness:
and bathe our world in your light.

We pray with Mary,
who mothered the Son of God:
Hail, Mary . . .

In silence now,
we bring to God's love
the special needs and concerns
known to us individually.

Silence

Celebrant
With great joy, Father,
in the knowledge
that we can trust you unconditionally,
we offer you our prayers,
through Jesus Christ.
Amen.

Sixteenth Sunday of the Year

Like a good shepherd,
Jesus sees the needs of his people and always responds with love.

Celebrant
Knowing God's love and concern for us all,
let us settle ourselves in his presence
and pray to him now.

Reader
Recognising the brokenness and disunity
of Christ's Church,
we pray that he may draw us closer to one another
as we draw closer to him;
we pray for all our Christian brothers and sisters
in this neighbourhood,
and for all who are searching
for meaning in their lives.

Silence

The Lord is my shepherd:
there is nothing I shall want.

With the noise of global conflicts
and human deprivation
thundering in our ears,
with the questions and doubts clamouring,
we pray that the Lord may shepherd our humanness
and lead us in the secret places of the heart.

Silence

The Lord is my shepherd:
there is nothing I shall want.

With the statistics of family life
challenging our values,
and with the pressures to conform to norms
in conflict with God's will,
we pray for a sound and centred wisdom
in all our daily living and life choices.

Silence

The Lord is my shepherd:
there is nothing I shall want.

With the stressed and overburdened,
the overworked and the unemployed,
we pray for balanced lives;
for physical, mental and spiritual health;
for patience in times of trouble,
and direction in times of confusion.

Silence

The Lord is my shepherd:
there is nothing I shall want.

As we remember with love and gratitude
the lives of those who have died in faith,
we commend them to eternal rest in the Lord
and his unchanging affection.

Silence

The Lord is my shepherd:
there is nothing I shall want.

We pray with Mary,
whose Son became our Good Shepherd:
Hail, Mary . . .

God our Father loves us;
in this silence
we name our particular petitions.

Silence

Celebrant
Father, in the sure knowledge
of your promise to answer the prayers
of all who are faithful,
we offer you our cares and concerns,
through Jesus Christ.
Amen.

SEVENTEENTH SUNDAY OF THE YEAR

Out of God's riches,
a great crowd is fed and satisfied from a small offering of food.

Celebrant
Knowing that our loving God
supplies all our needs,
let us pray to him now
on behalf of the Church and the world.

Reader
We pray for the Church
with all its varied ministries;
for the youngest to the oldest baptised members;
for those of mellow faith
and those who struggle with doubts.

Silence

Loving Father:
give us today our daily bread.

We pray for the strength
of a new commitment within ourselves
to pray the news each day
and share the pain we read about,
longing for peace and justice
in a world tense with aggression
and distorted with selfishness.

Silence

Loving Father:
give us today our daily bread.

We pray that the Lord may work in,
and transform, our homes and our relationships.
In all our meetings and conflicts
and all differences of opinion
may we work to the glory of God.

Silence

Loving Father:
give us today our daily bread.

We pray for all who suffer
or are heavily burdened;
we pray for their comfort and refreshment,
wholeness and restoration,
but above all for the consciousness
of Christ's presence in their pain,
and his love for them.

Silence

Loving Father:
give us today our daily bread.

We pray for the faithful souls
entering by the gate of physical death
that they may have eternal life.

Silence

Loving Father:
give us today our daily bread.

We make our prayer with Mary,
who fed and clothed her precious Son:
Hail, Mary . . .

As God our Father listens with love,
we name those we know
who are in any particular need.

Silence

Celebrant
Father, your generosity draws us
to love more deeply;
hear us as we pray,
and use us in fulfilling our prayers.
We pray through Jesus Christ.
Amen.

EIGHTEENTH SUNDAY OF THE YEAR

*Jesus is the Bread of Life who satisfies our hunger
and sustains us on our journey to heaven.*

Celebrant
Let us pray to the God who loves us,
knows our needs, and provides for us.

Reader
As the travelling people of God,
we pray for a deepening hunger
for the things of God
and a loosening of our grip
on all the wants and expectations
which prevent us from moving forward God's way.

Silence

Feed us, Father:
with the Bread of Life.

As brothers and sisters with the whole of creation,
we pray for respect and reverence among people
regardless of wealth or status;
for responsible sharing of resources
and consideration for the natural world
of our fragile and beautiful planet.

Silence

Feed us, Father:
with the Bread of Life.

As we prepare and eat our food each day,
we pray for those who grow and manufacture it,
distribute and sell it, shop for it and cook it,
and for those with whom we share food.
May we all be built up with the spiritual feeding
which sustains us for ever.

Silence

Feed us, Father:
with the Bread of Life.

As we ask for daily bread,
we pray for those who are physically starving,
for all who hunger emotionally
or try to survive on spiritual junk food;
for those who mistrust God's feeding.

Silence

Feed us, Father:
with the Bread of Life.

As we remember with love
those who have journeyed through physical death,
we pray that, nourished by the Bread of Life,
they may travel on eagles' wings
into the brightness of eternal life.

Silence

Feed us, Father:
with the Bread of Life.

We pray now with Mary,
who so tenderly nurtured her holy child:
Hail, Mary . . .

Meeting our heavenly Father
in the stillness of silence,
let us bring to him
our own particular cares and concerns.

Silence

Celebrant
Father, we can never thank you enough
for what you have done for us,
and for the way you are transforming our lives;
with grateful hearts we offer you these prayers,
through Jesus Christ.
Amen.

Nineteenth Sunday of the Year

Just as bread is the visible form of life-giving nourishment,
so Jesus is the visible form of God's life-giving love.

Celebrant
Let us pray to our God
as we worship him in Spirit and in truth.

Reader
We pray for all who are commissioned and called
to work as leaders and prophets in the Church.
We pray for greater discernment
of the Lord's presence
and his will in our Christian communities,
and a clearing away of all that obscures our vision.

Silence

Heavenly Father, open our eyes:
to see your glory.

We pray against the cynicism
and complacency that deaden wonder.
In the ordinary things of life
may we detect love and wisdom;
through the everyday events
may we encounter Christ, walking alongside us.

Silence

Heavenly Father, open our eyes:
to see your glory.

We pray for breadwinners
and sandwich makers, and all food growers;
for the Spirit's presence in kitchens, dining rooms,
canteens, restaurants and bars;
wherever people gather to eat together.

Silence

Heavenly Father, open our eyes:
to see your glory.

We pray for those whose emotional damage
makes trusting and receiving
seem threatening and dangerous.
We pray for peace of mind for the anxious,
and hope for all who are close to despair.

Silence

Heavenly Father, open our eyes:
to see your glory.

We pray for those
who have reached the boundary of death,
that in faith they may journey through it
and out into the unconfined space
and joy of heaven.

Silence

Heavenly Father, open our eyes:
to see your glory.

We pray with Mary,
our spiritual Mother:
Hail, Mary . . .

Upheld by God's grace,
we pray now in silence
for any who specially need our prayer.

Silence

Celebrant
Father, we acknowledge
our total dependence on you,
and ask you to hear us as we pray,
through Jesus Christ.
Amen.

TWENTIETH SUNDAY OF THE YEAR

God's wisdom may appear foolishness
without the God-given grace to understand.

Celebrant
As we gather, conscious of our need of wisdom,
let us pray to our wise and loving God.

Reader
In all the decision-making,
problems and challenges of our church,
we ask for wise counsel and encouragement;
in all our worship and outreach.

Silence

Wise and loving God:
quieten us to hear your voice.

In all the clashes of needs and wants,
the half-forgotten hurts that drive aggression,
the half-remembered grievances,
barbed with revenge,
in all the world's raging and protesting,
we pray for the spirit of peace and reconciliation.

Silence

Wise and loving God:
quieten us to hear your voice.

In the daily batch of misunderstandings,
conflicting loyalties, negotiations and compromise,
may the Spirit walk among us
in our homes and places of work,
whispering sanity and mutual respect.

Silence

Wise and loving God:
quieten us to hear your voice.

For those engulfed by pain
or enslaved by addiction,
we pray for hope and healing;
may the Lord bless all those
whose minds think simply
and rely on others for basic care.

Silence

Wise and loving God:
quieten us to hear your voice.

May all who have left this life
in the Father's friendship
be gathered into his keeping for ever;
we pray too for those approaching death,
that they may know his love
surrounding them across time and eternity.

Silence

Wise and loving God:
quieten us to hear your voice.

We join our prayers with those of Mary,
whose spirit was always peaceful:
Hail, Mary . . .

Together in silence now,
we make our private petitions.

Silence

Celebrant
Most loving and merciful Father,
we ask you to take over our lives
and live through them,
and accept these our prayers
in the name of Jesus.
Amen.

TWENTY-FIRST SUNDAY OF THE YEAR

'To whom else could we go?
You alone have the words of eternal life.'

Celebrant
We have chosen to serve the Lord.
Let us pray to him now.

Reader
We pray for those whose faith
is being challenged or undermined
by inner doubts or outside influences.
We pray for those who build up our faith
and all who strive to proclaim the Gospel
in language that people understand.

Silence

Holy God, we believe:
help our unbelief.

We pray for our torn and fragmented world,
wrestling to equate the deep yearning for peace
with the instinctive urge
for gratification and power;
that many may have the courage
to walk God's way.

Silence

Holy God, we believe:
help our unbelief.

We pray for our loved ones;
for those who lift our hearts
and those who turn our hair grey.
We pray for those we instinctively warm to
and those with whom
there are frequent misunderstandings.

Silence

Holy God, we believe:
help our unbelief.

We pray for all who are marginalised,
scorned or rejected;
for those isolated through illness or imprisonment;
for those who feel that no one understands.
May the Lord surround them all with such love
that they may know they are precious.

Silence

Holy God, we believe:
help our unbelief.

We pray for those approaching death,
that through our prayers
they may know themselves
accompanied with love on that journey.
We pray for those who have died,
that they may come to know the full joy of heaven.

Silence

Holy God, we believe:
help our unbelief.

Now we join our prayers with those of Mary,
the Mother of Jesus:
Hail, Mary . . .

In silence, we name any we know
who especially need our prayer.

Silence

Celebrant
In great thankfulness
for all your blessings to us,
heavenly Father,
we offer you these prayers,
through Jesus Christ.
Amen.

TWENTY-SECOND SUNDAY OF THE YEAR

We need to be careful never to replace
the timeless commands of God with man-made traditions.

Celebrant
Our God is the source of all holiness;
with the needs of the Church and the world
close to our hearts,
let us pray to the only one
who can renew and redeem.

Reader
Aware of our temptation
to place our trust in rules and traditions,
we pray for a release in the Church
of such a desire to serve the living God
that nothing is allowed to get in the way of that.

Silence

Into your hands, O Lord:
we commit the future.

We recognise in ourselves
the universal dangerous wants and cravings
which are cultivated because they make money.
May we have such a loathing of evil
that there will be international co-operation
and individual responsibility in fighting it
and building one another up in love.

Silence

Into your hands, O Lord:
we commit the future.

May our homes, schools and churches
reflect and engender the Godly values
of mutual care, respect and responsibility,
of integrity and forgiveness.

Silence

Into your hands, O Lord:
we commit the future.

We stand alongside all who are hurting
in body, mind or spirit;
all who need courage, support or practical help.
May we be willing to become
part of God's answer
to our prayers for them.

Silence

Into your hands, O Lord:
we commit the future.

We commit to the Father's keeping
those who have died to this life;
that, freed from all pain, and forgiven,
they may live in the peace and joy of heaven.

Silence

Into your hands, O Lord:
we commit the future.

Encouraged by Mary's example of obedience,
we make our prayer with her:
Hail, Mary . . .

As God's stillness fills our hearts,
we pray for our own particular needs and concerns.

Silence

Celebrant
Heavenly Father,
in your love and mercy hear our prayers,
through the mediation of Jesus Christ.
Amen.

TWENTY-THIRD SUNDAY OF THE YEAR

Jesus comes fulfilling the hope of healing to wholeness;
he shows that mercy has triumphed over judgement.

Celebrant
Let us pray to our loving and merciful God.

Reader
In gratitude for the richness and diversity
of each unique identity,
we pray for the separate members
of this Body of Christ, and our corporate nature,
that we may be filled at every level
with the living breath of God.

Silence

Father of mercy:
let your kingdom come.

In gratitude for the beauty and variety
of our landscapes and cultures, all over the world;
for starscapes and the wideness of space,
we pray that we may cherish and respect
this universe we inhabit,
and respect all those who look or sound
different from ourselves.

Silence

Father of mercy:
let your kingdom come.

In gratitude for the hope
each newborn child brings;
for the gentle gifts of laughter and friendship,
thoughtfulness and sympathy,
we pray that our eyes may see all others
with God's affection.

Silence

Father of mercy:
let your kingdom come.

In gratitude for the patient endurance
of so many who suffer so much,
we pray that they may come to know
Christ's wholeness and refreshing,
his upholding and healing.

Silence

Father of mercy:
let your kingdom come.

In gratitude for the promise of mercy
triumphing over judgement,
we commend to God's love for ever
our own loved ones who have died.

Silence

Father of mercy:
let your kingdom come.

We join our prayers with those of Mary,
who was full of compassion for others:
Hail, Mary . . .

In this silence,
we bring our particular petitions
to God our Father.

Silence

Celebrant
Father, your character is so rich in mercy;
please hear our prayers
which we offer in the name of Jesus.
Amen.

Twenty-fourth Sunday of the Year

Loving obedience to God is shown by Jesus
to be a quality rich in courage and wisdom,
a quality to be highly respected.

Celebrant
As sons and daughters of our heavenly Father,
responding to his call,
let us bring to him our needs and concerns.

Reader
That we may all learn to think God's way
and desire to do his will above everything else;
that we may be ready to suffer if necessary,
and put ourselves out, and do that cheerfully,
considering it a privilege.

Silence

Lord, in the spirit of obedience:
we ask your guidance.

That the craving to be most powerful
may be transformed into a yearning
for mutual respect and harmony;
that wealth may not shout louder than right,
and the whisper of truth may be heard
above the clamour of expediency.

Silence

Lord, in the spirit of obedience:
we ask your guidance.

That within our homes and places of work
we may practise self-discipline in all that we say,
and in the way it is said,
using our mouths to speak wisely and positively
with love in both hearts and voices.

Silence

Lord, in the spirit of obedience:
we ask your guidance.

That those whose bodies or spirits
are heavy with suffering
may be given courage and hope,
ease from the pain, and healing to wholeness.
That we may know how best to help them.

Silence

Lord, in the spirit of obedience:
we ask your guidance.

That those who have died in faith
may rise to eternal life,
and that we may so live on earth
that we are all prepared
for meeting the Father face to face in heaven.

Silence

Lord, in the spirit of obedience:
we ask your guidance.

We make our prayer with Mary,
Mother of Jesus, the Christ:
Hail, Mary . . .

In the knowledge
that God our Father hears us,
let us name our own particular petitions.

Silence

Celebrant
Father of mercy, hear our prayers
which we offer through Jesus, the Christ.
Amen.

TWENTY-FIFTH SUNDAY OF THE YEAR

*The truly great in God's eyes are those
who are prepared to be last of all and servant of all.*

Celebrant
Let us pray to the God of glory
in whom we live and move and have our being.

Reader
We pray that the Church may hold true
to the teaching of Jesus,
free from the worldly values of status and ambition.
We pray for a spirit of humility
to deflate all pomposity and arrogance.

Silence

Yours, Lord, is the kingdom:
yours the power and yours the glory.

We pray that all in positions of power,
authority and influence in our world
may recognise their calling to servanthood
and never lose their identity
with the needs and longings of those they serve.

Silence

Yours, Lord, is the kingdom:
yours the power and yours the glory.

We pray that all communities
may look after one another,
supporting the vulnerable, encouraging the timid,
providing practical help for all who need it,
and nurturing the young in a climate of trust.

Silence

Yours, Lord, is the kingdom:
yours the power and yours the glory.

We pray that none may be considered expendable,
or beyond our cherishing;
we pray for all who have lost heart,
through pain, suffering or sin,
that God's redeeming power may work its wonders
in the very darkest situations.

Silence

Yours, Lord, is the kingdom:
yours the power and yours the glory.

We pray that all who have wearily
struggled to death
may know the joy of burdens laid down,
and new, lasting life transforming them
through the eternal love of God.

Silence

Yours, Lord, is the kingdom:
yours the power and yours the glory.

We make our prayer with Mary,
who shared her Son's sorrows:
Hail, Mary . . .

Trustingly, we pray in silence
to our loving Lord,
who considers each one of us special.

Silence

Celebrant
Father, you always give us far more
than we can ever deserve;
please fulfil our prayers
in the way that is best for us.
We ask in the name of Jesus Christ.
Amen.

TWENTY-SIXTH SUNDAY OF THE YEAR

*Don't let your body lead you into sin
and risk exchanging eternal life for eternal punishment.*

Celebrant
Conscious of our need for God's power
in our lives, our Church and our world,
let us pray to him now.

Reader
We pray for the courage
to reject sin and evil in our own lives.
May our churches be powerhouses of the Spirit,
training and upholding us
as we live the Father's life and love in the world.

Silence

Your Law, O Lord, is perfect:
it revives the soul.

We pray for a greater awareness
of what damages souls and encourages evil,
and for widespread commitment
to addressing the dangers.
We pray for all who earn their living
through selling what destroys lives.

Silence

Your Law, O Lord, is perfect:
it revives the soul.

We pray for the young,
and the vulnerable in every community,
for all in positions of trust,
for child-minders, playgroups and schools,
for loving nurture and protection from all evil.

Silence

Your Law, O Lord, is perfect:
it revives the soul.

We pray for all long-term carers
and those they look after,
for all who are having
to learn dependence gracefully,
and those who are imprisoned by their guilt.
May the Lord work his healing love in them all,
reassuring them of his presence.

Silence

Your Law, O Lord, is perfect:
it revives the soul.

We pray that no one may be lost eternally,
that all may turn from their sin
and trust in God's mercy;
that physical death may be but the gate to heaven.
We commend to God's loving mercy
those who have recently died.

Silence

Your Law, O Lord, is perfect:
it revives the soul.

Encouraged by Mary's steadfast example,
we make our prayer with her:
Hail, Mary . . .

In silence filled with love,
we name our particular prayer burdens.

Silence

Celebrant
With thankfulness and praise
for all your blessings to us, Father,
we offer you these prayers,
through Jesus Christ.
Amen.

TWENTY-SEVENTH SUNDAY OF THE YEAR

*Human beings are made responsible for the care of creation
but are subject to God in all aspects of their lives.*

Celebrant
Let us come before God our Maker,
making our prayers to him,
through Jesus and in the power of the Holy Spirit.

Reader
We pray that the Church may be alive
to God's beckoning,
quick to obey his will
and always ready to act in his loving service
for the good of the world.

Silence

Lord of heaven:
let your will be done.

We pray that all leaders and heads of state
may take wise advice and act responsibly
for the well-being of all.
We pray for God's guidance
in the way we manage and care for this planet,
its resources, riches and inhabitants.

Silence

Lord of heaven:
let your will be done.

We pray for all marriages,
for those seeking marriage partners
and those whose marriages are under strain.
We pray for all in close relationships,
that there may be mutual love and respect.

Silence

Lord of heaven:
let your will be done.

We pray for all who are suffering
through illness, accident or deliberate cruelty;
for refugees and all who are abused;
that through the caring of human hands
they may experience the caring hands of God.

Silence

Lord of heaven:
let your will be done.

We pray for all who have died violently
or suddenly, or with no one to miss them.
May all who have died in faith
be judged with mercy
and welcomed into eternal life.

Silence

Lord of heaven:
let your will be done.

We pray with Mary,
the Mother of the Lord:
Hail, Mary . . .

Knowing that God our Father
hears the cries of his children,
we pray in silence
for our needs and cares.

Silence

Celebrant
Father of compassion and mercy,
accept our prayers,
through the person of Jesus Christ.
Amen.

TWENTY-EIGHTH SUNDAY OF THE YEAR

The most valuable possession
is not the wealth that owns us, but is Christ,
the Wisdom of God, who gives us untold riches.

Celebrant
Let us lay down our own agendas
and seek the face of God,
and his will for the Church and for the world.

Reader
We pray for all who are seeking God,
and for the nurturing process in this parish.
We pray for opportunities to share God's love
and draw others to meet him.

Silence

Father, your will be done:
on earth as in heaven.

We pray for all who are fighting against evil
for goodness, truth and justice,
both those who make the world news
and those whose battles are known only to God.
We pray for our country and its leaders,
that this nation may seek God.

Silence

Father, your will be done:
on earth as in heaven.

We pray that wealth and comfort may not divert us
from searching out the heart of God;
that we may hear God's challenging
and gladly respond to him;
that our homes and communities
may sparkle with God's glory.

Silence

Father, your will be done:
on earth as in heaven.

We pray for the disillusioned and depressed
and all who have lost their way in life;
we pray for those corrupted by evil,
trained in hatred and twisted by bitterness.
We pray for the transforming of these lives.

Silence

Father, your will be done:
on earth as in heaven.

We pray for those whose earthly life
has come to an end,
and for those who mourn their going.
May the dead rest in the peace and joy of heaven.

Silence

Father, your will be done:
on earth as in heaven.

We join our prayer with Mary,
who laid up treasure in heaven:
Hail, Mary . . .

As our loving Father listens in love,
we share with him our personal burdens,
joys and sorrows.

Silence

Celebrant
Father, in your great mercy,
hear these prayers we offer,
through Jesus Christ.
Amen.

Twenty-ninth Sunday of the Year

*Even the Son of Man himself came not to be served
but to serve, and to give his life as a ransom for many.*

Celebrant
In humility and love, let us pray together
to the God of our making and redeeming.

Reader
That all Christians may fulfil their vocation
to be servants, caring for the needs of others,
obedient to their Lord in all things
and supportive of one another
in worship, prayer and deepening faith.

Silence

Into your hands, O Lord:
we commit our prayers.

That those who govern and advise
may seek out God's will
and the good of all
in each crisis, dilemma and debate.

Silence

Into your hands, O Lord:
we commit our prayers.

That we may develop the habit
of rejoicing in the opportunities to serve,
and to put ourselves out for others,
laying down our craving for praise
and importance.

Silence

Into your hands, O Lord:
we commit our prayers.

That those who suffer in mind, body and spirit
may sense the Christ close beside them,
knowing his healing and resting in his love.

Silence

Into your hands, O Lord:
we commit our prayers.

That those who have died in faith
may be welcomed into the light of heaven,
and that all who are walking in sin today
may turn away from evil, and live.

Silence

Into your hands, O Lord:
we commit our prayers.

We pray with Mary,
who knew the reality of suffering:
Hail, Mary . . .

God our Father loves us;
in silence now,
we bring our personal petitions to him.

Silence

Celebrant
Father, in your unfailing mercy,
we ask you to accept these prayers,
through Jesus Christ.
Amen.

Thirtieth Sunday of the Year

In Jesus, God gathers his scattered people and opens their eyes to see.

Celebrant
As children of our heavenly Father,
trusting in his will and capacity to care for us all,
let us pray.

Reader
We pray for all pastoral care in the Church,
for the ministries of listening and counselling;
the sharing of grief; the freeing from guilt.
We pray for the grace to accompany
others to Christ's healing love.

Silence

What do you want God to do for you?
Lord, we want to see.

We pray for the healing of the nations;
for a recognition of our need of God
and a turning away from all that is evil.
We pray for all in authority and worldly power,
that they may be guided along right paths.

Silence

What do you want God to do for you?
Lord, we want to see.

We pray for an increase in love for one another,
that we may be better at recognising needs
and responding to them;
that we may give more time to those we love.

Silence

What do you want God to do for you?
Lord, we want to see.

We pray for those who are blind
or partially sighted,

and those who are spiritually or emotionally blind.
We pray for the opening of eyes to see God's way
and faith to trust him through good and ill.

Silence

What do you want God to do for you?
Lord, we want to see.

We pray for those whose eyes
have shut to this world,
that they may open to the brightness
and joy of heaven.

Silence

What do you want God to do for you?
Lord, we want to see.

We pray with Mary,
whose spiritual vision was clear:
Hail, Mary . . .

To God, our heavenly Father,
we pray for our own intentions.

Silence

Celebrant
Father,
you pour out your blessings so richly on us;
with thankful hearts we praise you,
and ask you to hear our prayers,
through Jesus Christ.
Amen.

Thirty-first Sunday of the Year

To love the living God with heart, soul and strength,
and to love our neighbour as ourselves
means far more than any sacrificial offerings.

Celebrant
As God's people, gathered in his presence,
let us pray.

Reader
For all who preach and teach the Gospel
in word and sacrament
throughout the worldwide Church.
For those who lead prayer groups
and Bible studies,
and all who gossip their faith to others.

Silence

O Lord our God:
in you we trust.

For all who are tortured or persecuted
for what they believe;
for the voiceless and powerless,
for the powerful and coercive.

Silence

O Lord our God:
in you we trust.

For greater respect for one another
as children of God's making;
for God's presence in each conversation,
discussion and debate,
each concern and celebration.

Silence

O Lord our God:
in you we trust.

For healing and wholeness,
mending and comforting,
calming and refreshing,
wherever lives and bodies ache.

Silence

O Lord our God:
in you we trust.

For everlasting peace in the arms of God
for those who have come to the end
of their life on earth
and comfort for all who grieve.

Silence

O Lord our God:
in you we trust.

Mary faithfully loved God and her neighbour;
let us join our prayers with hers:
Hail, Mary . . .

In the silence of our hearts,
we pray for any needs known to us personally.

Silence

Celebrant
Father, with grateful hearts for the gift of life,
we offer you these prayers,
together with ourselves
for your service;
in Jesus' name we pray.
Amen.

THIRTY-SECOND SUNDAY OF THE YEAR

Loving generosity is the hallmark of Godly giving.

Celebrant
Let us pray to our loving and generous God.

Reader
We pray that God will transform our giving
and provide us with the courage
to renounce all meanness of spirit,
until we are glad to give freely and lovingly.

Silence

Give us today our daily bread:
give us – and forgive us.

We pray that we may be good stewards
of this planet we are given to inhabit;
that all may learn to share what we have here
and look after it well for those who come after us.

Silence

Give us today our daily bread:
give us – and forgive us.

We pray that we may be more generous
in the attention we give to one another;
in allowing others to be themselves,
different from us but just as valid.

Silence

Give us today our daily bread:
give us – and forgive us.

We pray for the poor and for the rich,
for all whose lives are somehow impoverished.
We pray for those in debt
and all who are finding finances a great worry.

Silence

Give us today our daily bread:
give us – and forgive us.

We pray for those who have died,
that in God's mercy they may be welcomed
into the peace and joy of heaven.

Silence

Give us today our daily bread:
give us – and forgive us.

We join our prayers with those of Mary,
who gave of herself without stinting:
Hail, Mary . . .

In quietness now,
we pray for our own particular needs
and concerns.

Silence

Celebrant
Father, we thank you for bringing us here today,
and ask you to accept our prayers
through Jesus Christ.
Amen.

THIRTY-THIRD SUNDAY OF THE YEAR

We are to be on our guard; great anguish will accompany the last days,
but all that is good and loving, wise and true
will be saved and celebrated for ever.

Celebrant
As God's love has drawn us, let us pray.

Reader
That the Church may grow and flourish,
protected from evil within and without;
that in worship and ministry
God's love may be brought into places of darkness
and offer many the light of hope.

Silence

Lord our God:
show us the path of life.

That our shrinking world
may bring about co-operation
and a fresh appreciation of one another's cultures;
that we may encourage one another
in goodness, peace and love.

Silence

Lord our God:
show us the path of life.

That we may take time
to cherish our loved ones in the present moment,
and value the blessings we receive each day.

Silence

Lord our God:
show us the path of life.

That God's healing touch
may bring wholeness and peace

to those who suffer,
and hope to those who are close to despair.

Silence

Lord our God:
show us the path of life.

That God's love may surround those
travelling through death
and bring them safely to heaven.

Silence

Lord our God:
show us the path of life.

We pray now with Mary,
who showed us how to wait
with a quiet heart:
Hail, Mary . . .

As God's stillness fills our hearts,
we make our private petitions.

Silence

Celebrant
Trusting in your promise to hear us, Father,
we offer you these prayers,
through Jesus Christ.
Amen.

CHRIST THE KING

Jesus Christ is the everlasting King
whose kingdom is not of this world,
but grows in the hearts of his people and lasts for ever.

Celebrant
As children of the kingdom,
let us make our prayers to the eternal God,
who loves us.

Reader
We pray that the kingdom may come
in the worldwide communities
of those who believe in Jesus Christ –
may our lives enthrone him.

Silence

Spirit of the living God:
may your kingdom come.

We pray that the kingdom may come
in the nations of our world
and in their leadership;
for God's values to take root and grow;
for each person to be respected
as a beloved child of God.

Silence

Spirit of the living God:
may your kingdom come.

We pray that the kingdom may come
in our homes and families,
our neighbourhoods and places of work,
in all thinking, all speaking and all action.

Silence

Spirit of the living God:
may your kingdom come.

We pray that the kingdom may come
in all hospitals and surgeries,
and in every place of pain and sadness.

Silence

Spirit of the living God:
may your kingdom come.

We pray that the kingdom may come
in the final stages of earthly life,
in the journey through death,
and in the awakening to eternal life.

Silence

Spirit of the living God:
may your kingdom come.

We make our prayer with Mary,
Mother of Christ the King:
Hail, Mary . . .

The God of Peace is listening;
in this silence,
we name those we know
who are in any particular need.

Silence

Celebrant
Most merciful and loving Father,
we ask you to hear and answer our prayers
which we offer in the name of Jesus.
Amen.

MARY, MOTHER OF GOD – 1 JANUARY

Jesus Christ, the Son of God, is born of a woman.

Celebrant
Let us still our bodies and souls
as we gather to pray to the God
who made us and loves us.

Reader
As the Church we are the Body of Christ;
we thank you, Lord God, for Mary's mothering
which we share with Jesus.
We thank you for her love and faithfulness
and her example of willing co-operation.

Silence

Your will, Lord:
be done in us.

Out of love for the world
God sent his Son into the world;
we pray for all who live in the darkness of sin,
for the places where evil and corruption flourish,
where the problems and troubles
seem almost too entrenched to be solved.
We pray for hearts to be healed of hatred
and hope to be rekindled.

Silence

Your will, Lord:
be done in us.

As we remember with gratitude
Mary's mothering in the home at Nazareth,
we pray for our own homes and families,
for all expectant mothers,
those giving birth and the children being born,
that they may be surrounded and upheld
with love and affection.

Silence

Your will, Lord:
be done in us.

As we call to mind those we know
who are in trouble, need or sorrow,
we pray for comfort and healing,
refreshment and encouragement.

Silence

Your will, Lord:
be done in us.

We thank you, Lord God, that through the cross,
death no longer has the victory;
we pray for those mothers who have died to this life
that they may know the fullness of joy in heaven.

Silence

Your will, Lord:
be done in us.

We pray with Mary,
our spiritual mother:
Hail, Mary . . .

Meeting our heavenly Father
in the stillness of silence,
let us whisper to him
our particular burdens of prayer.

Silence

Celebrant
Father, we bring these prayers
through Jesus Christ, our Saviour.
Amen.

THE PRESENTATION OF THE LORD (CANDLEMAS) – 2 FEBRUARY

In accordance with Jewish tradition,
the Light of the World is presented as a first-born baby
in the temple at Jerusalem.

Celebrant
As we gather in Christ's name,
let us bring to mind those
who particularly need our prayer support.

Reader
We remember those who teach the faith
throughout the Church and throughout the world.
Keep them close to your guiding,
and open the hearts of those they teach
to hear and receive your truth.

Silence

Show us your ways:
and help us to walk in them.

We remember those in positions
of authority and influence
in this country and in all societies,
that needs may be noticed and addressed,
good values upheld and all people respected.

Silence

Show us your ways:
and help us to walk in them.

We remember those who looked after us
when we were very young,
and those who have no one to love and care for them.
We remember all young families
and all the children in our parish,
that they may be introduced to the one true God
and live their lives in his company.

Silence

Show us your ways:
and help us to walk in them.

We remember the elderly faithful
and especially those who are housebound
and can no longer join us to worship in person.
We thank you for their example
and ask you to increase our love for one another
across the age groups.

Silence

Show us your ways:
and help us to walk in them.

We remember those who have finished
their lives on earth
and commit them to your everlasting care
and protection.
We ask you to keep us faithful to the end of our life.

Silence

Show us your ways:
and help us to walk in them.

We offer our prayers with Mary
who took on the joys and sorrows
of mothering Jesus:
Hail, Mary . . .

In silence, let us bring to our God
the concerns of our own hearts,
knowing his love for us all.

Silence

Celebrant
Father, through the light of life
we are enabled to pray,
in the assurance of your faithfulness.
We offer our prayers
through Christ, the Light of the World.
Amen.

SAINT JOHN THE BAPTIST – 24 JUNE

*John is born with a mission to prepare the way
for the Messiah by calling people to repentance.*

Celebrant
Let us pray together in the presence of God.

Reader
Father, into every situation of doubt
and despondency among your followers
breathe your faithfulness.

Silence

Prepare us, O Lord:
to walk in your ways.

Father, into our strongholds of ambition
and defensiveness
breathe your humility.

Silence

Prepare us, O Lord:
to walk in your ways.

Father, into the prisons of guilt and revenge
breathe the grace of forgiveness.

Silence

Prepare us, O Lord:
to walk in your ways.

Father, into the darkness of pain and fear
breathe your reassurance.

Silence

Prepare us, O Lord:
to walk in your ways.

Father, into our complacency
breathe your zeal.

Silence

Prepare us, O Lord:
to walk in your ways.

Father, into our homes and places of work
breathe your fellowship and love.

Silence

Prepare us, O Lord:
to walk in your ways.

Father, into the whole of your creation
breathe your joy and peace.

Silence

Prepare us, O Lord:
to walk in your ways.

We make our prayer with Mary,
who rejoiced with her cousin Elizabeth
over the birth of John the Baptist:
Hail, Mary . . .

In silence, let us bring our private prayers
to the loving mercy of God.

Silence

Celebrant
Father, like John the Baptist,
may we courageously prepare the way
for the coming of the kingdom.
Through Christ, our Lord.
Amen.

SAINTS PETER AND PAUL – 29 JUNE

Through the dedication of the apostles Peter and Paul,
the Gospel of Jesus Christ spread and the Church was rapidly established.

Celebrant
Gathered as the Church of God,
let us pray.

Reader
Heavenly Father, as we celebrate
the life and work of Peter and Paul,
we give you thanks for our Church
and its faithfulness through the ages.
We ask your blessing on the Pope
and all leaders, pastors and teachers in the Church,
that they may be always open and attentive
to your guiding Spirit.

Silence

In all things, Father:
may your will be done.

Heavenly Father, as we recall the opposition
and persecution experienced by Peter and Paul,
we pray for all who are persecuted and threatened
for their faith today,
and for those working to discredit and crush
the influence of the Church.
We pray for the leaders of the nations
and those who advise and support them,
that they may seek what is right and good,
and bear in mind the needs of those they serve.

Silence

In all things, Father:
may your will be done.

Heavenly Father, we pray
that in our daily prayers and conversations,
our daily work and service,
we may remain true to your teaching

and love with your compassion,
whatever the cost.

Silence

In all things, Father:
may your will be done.

Heavenly Father, we pray for all who are imprisoned,
whether physically, emotionally or spiritually;
free them to live in the freshness of your love
and the security of your faithfulness.

Silence

In all things, Father:
may your will be done.

Heavenly Father, as we recall with gratitude
the willingness of Peter and Paul
to risk their lives in your service,
we pray for all who have died in faith
and thank you for their love and commitment.
Welcome them into your eternity;
may they know your peace and joy for ever.

Silence

In all things, Father:
may your will be done.

We join our prayers
with those of Mary our Mother:
Hail, Mary . . .

In the stillness of God's peace,
we bring our personal prayers
to our loving Father.

Silence

Celebrant
Father, accept these prayers
for the Church and for the world;
we pray that in all things
your kingdom may come.
Through Jesus Christ our Lord.
Amen.

The Transfiguration of the Lord – 6 August

*Jesus is seen in all God's glory,
and as fulfilling the Law and the prophets.*

Celebrant
Let us quieten ourselves
in the presence of the living God,
as we pray.

Reader
Father, you know us better than we know ourselves,
and are well aware of the needs
and pains in your Church.
We lift them now to your healing love.

Silence

Father, we love you:
open our eyes to see your glory.

In our world there are decisions to be made,
countries to be governed and people to be honoured.
We lift them now to your grace and wisdom.

Silence

Father, we love you:
open our eyes to see your glory.

In our neighbourhood and in our homes
there are celebrations and tragedies,
times of hope, weariness and tenderness.
We lift them now to your parenting.

Silence

Father, we love you:
open our eyes to see your glory.

In our hospitals and clinics there are many in pain,
many who are fearful,
and many who have lost hope.
We lift them now to your comfort and protection.

Silence

Father, we love you:
open our eyes to see your glory.

As each day others die and enter your presence,
we ask your mercy
and commend them to your safe keeping.

Silence

Father, we love you:
open our eyes to see your glory.

We pray with Mary
who saw in her Son the glory of God:
Hail, Mary . . .

Let us be still and silent in God's presence
and pray in faith to our loving Father.

Silence

Celebrant
Father, as the disciples saw your glory
revealed in Jesus,
so may your glory be revealed in us.
Through Christ our Lord.
Amen.

THE ASSUMPTION – 15 AUGUST

The Almighty has done great things for me!

Celebrant
As children of our heavenly Father,
let us gather ourselves to pray.

Reader
Lord our God, on this feast of the Assumption,
we praise and thank you
for the mothering love of Mary,
Mother of Christ and his Body, the Church.
We pray for each member of the Church of God,
both lay and ordained,
in their ministry to encourage one another
as loving servants to the needs of the world.

Silence

Lord of life:
may your kingdom come.

We pray for the world Christ died to save,
with its diversity of cultures and beliefs,
expectations and memories,
and its shared resources and human needs;
we pray for those who lead and govern,
for responsible stewardship
and wise decision-making.

Silence

Lord of life:
may your kingdom come.

We pray for our parents and our own families,
for all those we love and all who love us;
we pray for our friends and neighbours,
our colleagues, employers and employees;
we pray for those on either side of us now.

Silence

Lord of life:
may your kingdom come.

We pray for those who are in pain,
sorrow or distress,
that they may know your presence
and receive your comfort and healing.

Silence

Lord of life:
may your kingdom come.

We pray for those who have died
and all who grieve for them;
we pray for those dying alone and unnoticed,
we pray for those dying unwanted and unborn.

Silence

Lord of life:
may your kingdom come.

We pray with Mary,
our Mother in heaven:
Hail, Mary . . .

In the silence of eternity,
let us bring to our loving Father
the concerns on our own hearts.

Silence

Celebrant
Father, with Mary we know
that you give us abundant blessing;
hear these prayers in mercy and love.
Through Christ our Lord.
Amen.

THE TRIUMPH OF THE HOLY CROSS – 14 SEPTEMBER

Through Christ's loving obedience,
even to death on a cross, he has opened up
the way for us to eternal life.

Celebrant
In the knowledge of the extent of God's love for us,
let us pray.

Reader
Father, we pray for all in your Church
whose journey through life is hard,
dangerous, exhausting or confused.

Silence

Lord of love:
you have won the victory.

We pray for those whose lives
are disrupted, oppressed or devastated
by war, famine or political unrest.

Silence

Lord of love:
you have won the victory.

We pray for our families, friends and neighbours;
all who cause us concern
and all in need of your peace.

Silence

Lord of love:
you have won the victory.

We pray for those whose lives
are filled with pain, resentment or hatred;
for all who are trapped in addiction or despair.

Silence

Lord of love:
you have won the victory.

We pray for those who have died
and for those who miss them;
we thank you for saving us through the cross
so that we can hope to share the glory of heaven.

Silence

Lord of love:
you have won the victory.

We join our prayers with those of Mary,
who witnessed the tragedy
and the triumph of the cross:
Hail, Mary . . .

As we kneel at the foot of the cross,
trusting in its power to save,
let us bring to the Lord our own prayers.

Silence

Celebrant
Father, you gave us the gift of your Son;
accept these prayers and transform our lives.
Through Christ our Lord.
Amen.

ALL SAINTS – 1 NOVEMBER

Lives that have shone with God's love on earth
are filled with joy as they see their Lord face to face.

Celebrant
Knowing our dependence on God in all things,
let us pray to him now.

Reader
Glorious God, as we celebrate the lives
of those Church members who have shone
with the brightness of your love,
we offer you ourselves and our lives in fresh commitment
and conscious awareness of our need for you
in this parish and as individual Christians.

Silence

Just as I am:
I come.

Powerful God, may your kingdom of love and peace
be established in this world and grow.
We pray for both the influential and the ignored,
both the popular and the disliked,
both the ambitious and the vulnerable.
Teach us all your ways and your values.

Silence

Just as I am:
I come.

Loving God, we call to mind
our families and friends, neighbours and colleagues,
thanking you for all the loving care and forgiveness,
and asking your light to shine
in all areas of hurt and misunderstanding.

Silence

Just as I am:
I come.

Healing God, we bring to you
those whose lives are darkened by pain, fear or weariness.

Come to our aid; help us to bear what must be carried,
and take from us all resentment and bitterness,
replacing it with the abundance of peace.

Silence

Just as I am:
I come.

Eternal God, we thank you for all the saints –
those recognised by the Church
and those known only to a few, and to you.
We praise you for their example and rejoice that they live in your heaven
with every tear wiped away.
In your mercy may all who have died in your friendship
know your lasting peace.

Silence

Just as I am:
I come.

Gracious God, you can take us as we are
and transform us by your life in us.
Clear our lives of all that is not of you, so that we let your goodness
shine through the colours of our personalities
and gifts you have given us.

Silence

Just as I am:
I come.

We join our prayers with those of Mary
and all the saints:
Hail, Mary . . .

In a time of silence
and in the presence of all the saints in heaven,
let us pray for our particular concerns.

Silence

Celebrant
Father, as we celebrate the joy of those
whose wills are united with yours,
we commend to you our lives
and our hope of heaven,
through Christ our Lord.
Amen.

Feasts of the Dedication of a Church

The church building symbolises the spiritual temple,
being built of the living stones of God's people.

Celebrant
Gathered as the Church of Christ in this place,
let us pray together in his name.

Reader
Father, we give you thanks for this church building
and the privilege of worshipping you without fear.
We thank you for all
who have prayed and ministered here,
and ask that you keep us attentive to your voice,
worshipping you in spirit and in truth.

Silence

Take us, Lord:
renew us and use us.

Father, we pray for this area and its problems,
for all who live, work and raise their families here.
We thank you for all that is good and hopeful,
and ask you to bless and guide those in authority.

Silence

Take us, Lord:
renew us and use us.

Father, may the homes we represent
and all the homes of this parish
be filled with your light and love,
your warmth and welcome,
your comforting and peace.

Silence

Take us, Lord:
renew us and use us.

Father, may all who come to this place
in distress of body or soul
find here your healing and refreshment,
and touch the beauty of your holiness.

Silence

Take us, Lord:
renew us and use us.

Father, we commend to your love
all those who have worshipped here in the past,
both those we remember
and those known only to you.

Silence

Take us, Lord:
renew us and use us.

We make our prayers with Mary,
the Mother of the Church:
Hail, Mary . . .

In a time of silence, filled with God's peace,
we bring our personal prayers and petitions,
in the assurance of God's love.

Silence

Celebrant
Father, hear these prayers
which we offer as your people,
and build us as living stones
into a spiritual temple.
Through Christ our Lord.
Amen.

42000
9-99